HOW TO <u>LIVE</u>
365 DAYS A YEAR

HOW TO LIVE 365 DAYS A YEAR

by

JOHN A. SCHINDLER, M.D.

Chairman Department of Medicine
The Monroe Clinic
Monroe, Wisconsin

PRENTICE-HALL, INC.
Englewood Cliffs, N. J.

**THIS BOOK IS DEDICATED
TO THE UNSUNG MAGNIFICENCE
OF ORDINARY PEOPLE**

who, from paleolithic caves to modern assembly lines, have shown the *courage to endure* and the *determination to make the best of it.*

The courage to endure has helped people through woe piled on woe, defeat added to defeat, difficulty after difficulty. The determination to make the best of it has answered the dirges of ill winds with lilting, jigging tunes; has illuminated dark moments with cheerful, hopeful quips; has helped people grow better as situations grow worse.

To these two magnificent qualities in people this book is humbly dedicated, in the hope that it may be able to help, even a little, those who have forgotten that they, too, have these same qualities.

I WISH TO THANK...

I wish to thank the Editors of *The Progressive, The Reader's Digest, Science Digest, The Rotarian, The Wisconsin State Journal, The Milwaukee Journal,* and *The Chicago University Round Table* for permission to use portions of this book that they previously printed.

Especially do I wish to thank Professor H. B. McCarty, Rear Admiral Walter G. Schindler, U.S.N., Dr. Ben H. Brunkow, Professor Max Otto, Dr. Frederick Wellman, and Dr. Ralph D. Bennett, for giving of their time and valuable help in reading and suggesting changes in the manuscript.

Also I wish to thank the Honorable Alexander M. Wiley, United States Senate, Dr. Edgar S. Gordon, Dr. Burton Kintner, Dr. Millard Tufts, Mr. Henry Cox, Dr. Norman Vincent Peale, Dr. John Guy Fowlkes, and Mr. John English for their enthusiastic support and help in launching this book.

And most of all, I wish to thank my wife, Dorothea Schindler, for skillful editorial help, for never-failing inspiration and suggestion, and for an amazing understanding and patience over a period of three years during which the preparation of this book absorbed the few odd moments left over from a busy medical practice.

J.A.S.

CONTENTS

HOW TO <u>LIVE</u>
365 DAYS A YEAR

HOW WERE YOUR LAST 365 DAYS?

HOW WILL BE YOUR NEXT 365 DAYS?

➡ *For Most People, Living Consists in Muddling Through*

A great many people have lived on this earth since the human race began — billions and billions of them. And over every head, just as over yours and mine, has dangled the tempting word and idea called "Happiness." Happiness connotes a state that most people touch only momentarily, if at all, and that the majority (including the high, as well as the low) never attain in any fundamental way.

One of the big failures of the human race has been the failure of its members to attain anything like enduring happiness here on earth.

➡ *How Were Your Last 365 Days?*

To bring home what I mean, ask *yourself,* "How were *your* last 365 days?"

Were your last 365 days a thrilling series of gloriously alive moments? Were you running exhilaratingly and enthusiastically through a golden avenue of days, humming a happy tune, with never an apprehensive skip of a reluctant heart? How much of the time during your last 365 days were you occupied with cares (which is a mild term), or difficulties (which is a bit more severe), or troubles (which is frankly just what it means)?

Your last 365 days were probably not very different from anyone else's.

➤ *The Sad Reality in Most People's Lives*

Behind the front they put on for the public, most people are disturbed; many are perturbed; others are worried to the point of confusion; some are frankly frustrated. Most of them do not feel up to par; they have a tiredness, a pain, a disagreeable feeling, a misery. They have a dozen matters they are worried about. They are brimming with apprehensions, fears, irritations. They have never quite connected with good living. They have muddled through their last 365 days, trying to avoid but always managing to stumble over new, nagging troubles, never reaching healthy enthusiasms, but going along nibbling on constant cares, irritated more often than pleased, timorous more often than courageous, apprehensive more often than calm.

That is the sad failure of billions and billions of people who have passed across the earth.

The most important thing has not been learned: how to conduct ourselves so that we may *live*.

➡ *Your Life Can Be Good*

Human life — your life — need not be like that.

Your life *can* be an exhilarating and enthusiastic journey through a golden avenue of days, humming a happy tune. Actually, a life of that kind is just as easy, and infinitely better, than the old way of muddling through.

Living, instead of muddling through, is your reward for expending a very small amount of effort to attain know-how.

➡ *The Necessary Know-How for Living Can Be Yours*

In this Twentieth Century, for the first time in history, modern psychology and psychiatry have developed the know-how for *living*.

In this book, that new knowledge is presented in practical, usable terms. This book is specifically meant to teach people how to change their way of living from the way in which they conducted their last 365 days to a new way by which they can *live* during their next 365 days, and all their days thereafter.

➤ *The Method Used in This Book Has Had a Long, Successful Trial*

The method for *living* presented in this book has been gradually evolved through 20 years of effort, trial, error, and success, in a large mid-western medical clinic. It has proven very effective in helping thousands of people escape from the physical effects of muddled living and has given them a new know-how for going ahead on a new and better road.

➤ *The Connection Between Muddling Through and Most of Our Illness*

It is in the doctor's office that the almost universal failure to handle living effectively stands out in all its unfortunate complications.

People come to the doctor still wearing the front they always put on that says, "Except for these aches and pains, I am doing all right, of course. I'm conducting my living as satisfactorily as anyone can!"

But as the interview and examination proceed, it is evident that the strain of poor living, of muddling through, is most usually the cause of the person's illness.

➔ *We Humans Are Used to Enduring Unhappiness*

The patient doesn't come to the doctor about his *unhappiness,* which is actually the cause of his sickness. He makes no mention of his un-happiness until the doctor gains his confidence, and then he removes the front he is hiding behind.

The patient, even as you and I, has been toughened in a hard world. His is the attitude many people have always had: "Phooey! Happiness? This is a lovely word. But it's too bad! There isn't any! No one has ever really believed happiness exists, or ever will exist."

He accepts his unhappiness as an unfortunate, but normal, routine condition of life on earth.

➔ *But It Is Hard to Endure the Physical Symptoms of Unhappiness*

The patient comes to the doctor because of the *physical symptoms* that the strain of his muddling through has begun to produce, not because of his unhappiness. He is, of course, un-aware that his physical symptoms and unhappi-ness are both caused by the same muddling through.

He accepts the unhappiness as a matter of course.

But he doesn't accept the tiredness, the pain, and all manner of other symptoms. *They* are uncomfortable, and he is ready to do something about *them*.

He is amazed if he is told that the only effective thing he can do about them is to live differently, a concept that had not existed in his view of things. All of us think that the way we are living is the only way to live, under the circumstances.

But that is what the patient must learn to do — he must learn to live differently — to *live*. He must get rid of a lot of barnacles. He has only one alternative to continuing in his misery, and that is to quit producing emotional stress by muddling through and begin to make healthy emotions by knowing how to *live*.

➪ *Emotional Stress from Muddling Through Causes 50 Per Cent of Our Illness*

Laymen have only the vaguest impression that emotional stress causes *physical* disturbances. Most people have a very hazy idea of how frequently, and how profoundly, emotional stress affects the body.

Occasionally a person can be objective enough to see that his life is a sea of troubles, but he usually remains unaware that he is having any such thing as emotional stress. Emotional stress is a pretty intangible sounding thing to most people, and when their physical distress begins, they haven't the faintest idea that it is coming from their emotional stress.

The physical effects of the emotions lie outside consciousness or volition. Consciousness can control the changes of emotions only by changing the emotion potential of thought.

Everyone, and that includes you and me, underestimates both the extent and the effects of his emotional stress. As he muddles through his sea of trouble, everyone half-consciously prides himself on some sort of a vague control over such supposedly ephemeral matters as emotional stress.

Everyone has the idea, "This thing they call emotional stress may cause illness in some people, but you can bet your boots I'm not going to let it get *me!*"

But you can bet your boots the goblin will get him just the same.

And it will get *you,* "if you don't watch out!"

Virtually everyone does get emotionally induced illness at some time or other. *Over 50 per cent of all the illness that doctors see is emotionally induced illness!* That, my friend, is not an ephemeral situation. Expressed in monetary terms, that situation costs the United States many times more every year than the damage that would result if every river in the country were to go on an all-time high flood.

A situation of that kind is a national catastrophe!

And when emotional illness hits *you,* it's a personal catastrophe!

➡ *This Book Begins with an Explanation of Emotionally Induced Illness*

Most people, like yourself, are usually willing to go along unmindful of emotional stress until they learn, either the hard way or the smart way, that emotional stress eventually produces seri ous, disabling illness, and that *emotional stress is, today, our Number One cause of ill health.*

It is hard to shrug those facts off.

And so *How to Live 365 Days a Year* properly begins with an explanation of emotionally induced illness, because once you understand the miserable end results of emotional stress, you will understand the *necessity* of learning how to live.

➡ *Part I Describes Emotionally Induced Illness*

Part I of this book describes how the prevalent emotional currents in our lives cause the symptoms of the most remarkable, and by far the most common, physical disease we have.

This is a new field of knowledge, and as recently as 1936 the wildest imagination could not have surmised the tremendous effects that scientific research has since shown the emotions have upon our state of health.

In Part I the picture of emotional illness is painted with considerable completeness, in terms that do not bog the reader down in a morass of physiologic and medical jargon.

Chapter 1 is concerned with the question, "What, after all, is an emotion?"

You will be surprised to learn that an emotion, far from being an ephemeral sort of thing, is a very tangible affair that one can easily *observe* in the body. That's right! You can actually *see* an emotion.

The changes in the body that *are* the emotion are mediated partly through the stimulation of the *autonomic nervous system,* which is why emotionally induced illness has been called "It's your nerves."

But by far the most important emotional effects are produced through the action of the *endocrine glands,* of which the *pituitary gland,* situated at the base of the brain, is the most important. This role of the endocrine glands is a thrilling and almost unbelievable story that has been written since 1936, the year Dr. Hans Selye began his researches at Montreal University.

➽ *So What? What Are We Going to Do About It?*

The question naturally arises, "What are we going to do about muddled living, emotional stress, unhappiness, emotionally induced illness?"

How, in this world, is one to live in any other way than the way one *is* living?

➽ *Part II Provides the Answer for Emotional Stress from Muddling Through*

In Part II, this problem is reduced to the simple terms of a practical solution, a solution that is as easy to try as it is to understand.

The many varieties of help given us by modern psychiatry and psychology are leveled down to the common terms of daily life, and integrated into a one-two-three system for directing the course of your living from one minute to the next.

The method presented in Part II is essentially the same material my patients in the Monroe Clinic receive through private, illustrated talks and movies. As I said above, this method has gradually evolved out of many different approaches and attempts (varying all the way from group therapy to long ventilative sessions) to find a practical and successful way for patients to bring emotional *stasis* (that is, emotional tranquility; good adjustment) instead of emotional *stress* into their living. This method has proven to be very successful. Thousands of patients have found it a valuable guide to new heights in living they had never realized existed.

➡ *Immaturity Is the Cause of Muddling Through*

The problem boils down to this:

People conduct their lives so poorly, and have conducted their lives so poorly through all the ages, because no one has ever been taught how to grow up into fully rounded maturity. All of us, including the most dignified and responsible executive, fail to grow up in some important department of living or other; all of us continue to react to certain adult problems with childish reactions.

It is by trying to meet adult problems with childish reactions that we generate emotional stress.

➧ *There Is No Place Where People Are Taught Maturity*

People are not to be blamed for this universal failure to develop well-rounded maturity. Maturity does not come to a person naturally, like physical growth. Maturity is a cultural feature that must be learned.

There has been no organized attempt in our time, nor in any other time, to *teach* people the fundamentals of maturity.

➧ *The Family Does NOT Teach Maturity*

The average family has a negative influence on its members as far as developing maturity is concerned. Much of our emotional stress rises out of the common immaturities in family life. In fact, our families are our foremost cause of emotional stress, and, therefore, of ill health, in this country.

Chapter 10 reviews the common failures in families that cause stress in family members, and then presents a plan for successful family operation that will provide emotional maturity.

➧ *The Schools Do NOT Teach Maturity*

The schools do not as yet teach the student maturity. But educators are strongly interested in the problem; not only are they talking about it, but they are beginning to do something about it.

A textbook for teenagers like the one written by Judson and Mary Landis, *Building Your Life,* is a promising and exciting development.* This is the sort of thing that we need; such efforts are going to grow and develop, and in another decade or two our public schools will, doubtless, be doing a good job of teaching this most important aspect of living — maturity.

This new enterprise in education — teaching and grounding youth in the attitudes of maturity — will bring to human life a quality never attained and never dreamed of before. It will be more than a mere milestone in human progress: it will deserve to be classed as a millennium.

But until education becomes maturity-minded, the influences in our society for developing maturity are entirely haphazard. Fortunate is the person who falls under the influence of someone who managed to acquire maturity and who can pass it on to others — perhaps a parent, a teacher, a minister, a friend. Such fortune, however, remains haphazard

---

* Judson T. and Mary G. Landis, *Building Your Life* (New York: Prentice-Hall, Inc., 1954).

chance. Most people have no such good fortune and remain immature in essential fields of living and full of emotional stress.

➡ *Maturity Is a Matter of Attitudes*

Maturity is not a matter of being crammed full of technical or classical knowledge; nor does it consist in the ability to make important judgments correctly.

Maturity is essentially a collection of attitudes, attitudes that are more effective and helpful to the individual in meeting situations than are the attitudes a small child might have in the same situations. An attitude is an established way of reacting to certain classes of experiences.

The more mature a person is, the more complete is the stock of effective attitudes that he can bring to the great variety of experiences that arise in the course of living.

➡ *Maturity Includes Many Attitudes*

Throughout Part II the attitudes that comprise maturity are presented on the ground level of practical action, as obviously superior ways of handling the situations that are continually getting most people down.

There are several spots in life where the

possession of maturity is particularly important.

One such spot is the competitive field of modern business and industry, which is the subject of Chapter 12.

Another such spot is the domain of sex; here mature attitudes are particularly rare. Maturity in matters of sex is the subject of Chapter 11.

One of the most difficult spots in life has become the period of old age. Mature attitudes for meeting old age gracefully are the subject of Chapter 13.

➡ *There Is a Review at the End of Each Chapter*

To help the reader to review, or to go back to pick up a thread, each chapter is concluded with a brief review.

There may be even an occasional reader who is in such a hurry, or who feels himself rushing into emotionally induced illness at such a speed (the two really go together), that he will care to read only the chapter reviews. That is perfectly all right. If he absorbs what is in the reviews, he will be soothed and calmed in his hectic flight, and will find himself about to read the whole book after all. *Following that,* he can begin *living.*

➨ *The Last Chapter Is a Full Blueprint*

Chapter 15 is a blueprint of the chapter reviews in Part II, arranged in outline form so that the various items in the development of maturity can be correlated at a glance.

This outline will later serve the reader as a ready periodic review of the book's method for getting him out of the doldrums of muddling through and into the golden avenue of *living*.

➨ *This Is a Book for Everybody*

You will find that *How to Live 365 Days a Year* is not merely another of the variety known as "self-uplift" or "inspirational" books. The information and techniques presented in this book are something that everyone needs and that no one can live well without.

Not only is this book a way out of emotional stress, but it is a prevention for, or a way out of, emotionally induced illness.

For you, and for every man, this book has been written, so that you may avoid emotionally induced illness and may see a way to turn emotional stress into emotional health.

PART I. *HOW AND WHY EMOTIONALLY INDUCED ILLNESS OCCURS*

1. YOUR EMOTIONS PRODUCE MOST OF YOUR PHYSICAL DISEASE

Probably no greater confusion exists in this confused world than the one in the minds of nonmedical people concerning the type of illness loosely and erroneously described as "It's your nerves." This confusion in the lay mind is not remarkable at all, since until recently confusion also existed in the medical mind. We began as recently as 1936 to understand the mechanism by which a set of emotions could produce physical disease. The medical profession's education in the matter is just under way. Between the time the profession is educated in a subject and the time the lay population generally understands it, there is usually a lapse of 20 years. Thus we see that the educative process is in its early stages.

Functional disease, or emotionally induced illness, as it had best be called, is, every way you look at it, a very, very remarkable disease.

➤ *The Remarkable Prevalence of Functional Disease*

One of the outstanding things, for instance, about E. I. I.

(emotionally induced illness) is that over 50 per cent of those seeking medical aid today have it.

Put it differently: If *you* become ill tomorrow, or if *you* are ill today, the chances are a little better than 50-50 that you are ill with E. I. I.

Or, still another way of putting it: A big text book of medicine, such as medical students use, contains the account of roughly 1,000 different diseases that this human clay of ours is subject to. One of these diseases, emotionally induced illness, is as common as all the other 999 put together!

Perhaps it is a little hard for you, a layman, to believe these figures. But actually they are probably on the conservative side. A few years ago the Ochsner Clinic in New Orleans published a paper which stated that 74 per cent of 500 consecutive patients admitted to the department handling gastrointestinal diseases were found to be suffering from E. I. I. And in 1951, a paper from the Yale University Out-Patient Medical Department indicated that 76 per cent of patients coming to that Clinic were suffering from E. I. I.!

One naturally asks, "If this disease is so prevalent, why doesn't one hear more about it?" What's the answer? The answer is as peculiar as the disease itself.

➡ *Emotionally Induced Illness: The Dark Spot in Modern Medicine*

Everyone, including you and me, has had emotionally induced illness at some time or other. If you saw a physician when you had it, the chances are that the physician did not tell you what you had. There are two good reasons why he didn't.

The first reason is that although physicians have always known about the disease, and have been able to diagnose it for many years, it has been only in the last ten years that we have understood it well enough to begin to talk about it.

The second and most important reason the doctor did not

tell you what you had arises from the peculiar method by which this disease has been treated.

A doctor does not have to be in practice long to learn that merely telling a patient "You have nothing wrong with you; your trouble is being produced by your emotions," or "It's your nerves," is very poor therapy. It not only does the patient little or no good, but often angers him, sets him on the defensive, and sends him to another doctor. This one, with greater understanding of the patient's needs (not his condition), gives the patient the kind of a diagnosis he is willing to accept.

If a physician insists on using the frontal attack, and tells the patient that his trouble comes from his emotions, he must be prepared to follow up with an explanation of how the disease works to produce the patient's symptoms, what emotions are responsible for the patient's illness, and how the patient is to substitute better emotions for those he has been having. We call all this *adequate psychotherapy*. It is the only rational way we have had of treating E. I. I.

Drawbacks of adequate psychotherapy. But adequate psychotherapy, as it is understood today, is impossible — impossible because of TIME. The great obstacle to "adequate psychotherapy" is that it requires 20 hours per patient.

Using it, a doctor could, by working 20 hours a day, treat the equivalent of one patient a day. But the average doctor in this country sees 23 patients a day! Suppose the general doctor were to send these patients to psychiatric specialists. (I can hear some of you suggest that.) Giving adequate psychotherapy to the tremendous number of patients with E. I. I. would require several hundred thousand psychiatrists. There are only 5,000 at the present time in the United States. The problem of treating functional disease by "adequate" methods is thus, obviously, overwhelming. Less than 1 per cent of the patients with E. I. I. receive adequate psychotherapy by present standards.

Substitution therapy. The other 99 per cent of the patients with E. I. I. receive what might be termed "substitution therapy." This consists of giving the patient a substitute diagnosis that he can readily understand to be a cause of his illness, and then carrying on the treatment ostensibly for that cause. This is psychotherapy, too, but of a bastard variety.

Such substitution therapy has been the accepted treatment for thousands of years. The primitive witch doctor told his functional patient he was possessed with evil spirits. The treatment consisted in driving out the evil spirits by very dramatic and suggestive methods. I sometimes wish, when I have a tough patient, that I had a method of therapy half as suggestive as the one the witch doctor used.

The medieval doctor told his patient that he had an un-balance of the four humors and then proceeded to remove one — usually blood, because that was the easiest to remove.

The cultist of today tells his patient, "You have a vertebra out of place" and then makes passes purporting to put it back into place.

The modern physician uses modern substitute diagnoses such as *high or low basal metabolic rate, high or low blood pressure,* or *adrenal cortical insufficiency.* The last would make a hit in Park Avenue practice; but out in the grass roots country, a homely "sluggish liver" would get across much better and with much less fuss. Any *good* substitute diagnosis must be less severe than the disease the patient is afraid he had; otherwise, the diagnosis merely makes the patient sicker.

Substitution therapy has been possible through the ages because 60 per cent of the patients treated by almost *any* variety of substitution therapy feel improved for a period of two months. A patient improved for two months is a good advertisement for the substitution therapist. New patients are "sold" by the temporary improvement. It has made possible such substitution-therapeutic successes as the nostrums and quackeries for which the public annually spends billions of dollars. It is the functionally ill who buy these items, along with the billions of dollars of vitamin preparations that swamp the national market.

If the medical profession treated emotionally induced ill-ness as effectively as it does lobar pneumonia, the quacks would be out of business overnight. This disease is the bread and butter of both the physician and the irregular healer. If adequate methods of treatment were to banish it altogether, the cults and the marginal, lower-grade physician would vanish from the scene.

The worst feature of substitution therapy is that, in the long run, it makes the emotionally-ill person worse, and serves to cement the chronicity of the illness. Of the people treated by this method, only 8 per cent are any better at the end of one year. The others have added the name of another disease to their fear that they are not well. And where the doctor is not wise and careful in his substitute diagnosis, he may give the patient a very severe phobia of a serious illness. This kind of doctor-started disease is known in the profes-sion as an *iatrogenic illness,* meaning, in Greek, an illness started by a doctor. Three out of every five emotionally-ill patients I see in my office have an appreciable amount of iatrogenic illness, which makes treatment more difficult.

Large-scale efforts are under way to develop more rapid and more adequate methods of treating this disease that can be used by the general physician. It is safe to say that an-other 20 years will see a complete revolution in the treatment of this, our most common disease. This present dark spot of modern medicine will become as brightly illuminated as the rest of the medical map.

➤ Emotionally Induced Illness Is a Physical Disease

Let us distinctly understand that patients with this disease present themselves with *physical* symptoms, not *mental* symp-toms. This is a difficult point for the uninitiated to grasp.

The following is a partial list of the hundreds of symptoms this disease can produce. The percentage number after each symptom indicates how often its occurrence is due to emo-tionally induced illness.

From this partial list, you can get the idea that the common things people complain of are emotionally induced. But anyone in medical practice can tell you that most of the uncommon, bizarre symptoms are also usually caused by emotional troubles.

Complaint	Percentage
• Pain in the back of the neck	75
• Lump in the throat	90
• Ulcer-like pain	50
• Gall bladder-like pain	50
• Gas	$99\frac{44}{100}$
• Dizziness	80
• Headaches	80
• Constipation	70
• Tiredness	90

➡ *The More Intelligent You Are, the More You are Prone to E. I. I.*

Many people who do not understand the nature of the illness are apt to think that because of their own superior intelligence they are immune to emotionally induced illness. As a matter of fact, E. I. I. becomes more prevalent as one goes up the ladder of human responsibility, mental alertness and capacity.

This is probably because the alert mind can find ten things to be worried and concerned about in the time the unalert mind can think of only one. The person with greater mental capacity also takes on greater responsibilities, which means, usually, more tense emotions.

If "Intelligence" actually consisted of being intelligent, it would include, before anything else, the intelligent orientation and handling of the emotions. But apparently up to the present day this ability has been pretty generally left out of being intelligent, and the so-styled intelligent people are usually the ones least capable of guiding their emotions through the maze of everyday living.

The group in my part of the country who have emotionally induced illness *least* often are the farmers' wives with families of nine or ten who, in addition to their housework, also help out on the farm. Their minds are too busy with work to "think," and they are too busy taking care of other people to think of themselves.

One of these wonderful human beings told me one time when I asked her whether she ever got tired (one of the most common functional symptoms), "Son, 25 years ago, I taught myself never to ask myself that question." And that, incidentally, is the best cure for that kind of tiredness.

➤ *William James' Definition of an Emotion*

To understand emotionally induced illness one must, of course, understand what an emotion is. In 1884, emotion was defined by William James as "a state of mind that manifests itself by sensible changes in the body." With every emotion (and we are having some kind of an emotion every minute) changes are taking place in muscles, in blood vessels, in the viscera, in the endocrine glands. These changes and the perceptive mental state that accompanies them *are* the emotion. Without these bodily changes, there would be no emotion.

➤ *Two General Kinds of Emotions*

Although there are some minor exceptions, all emotions belong in one of two groups as far as the changes they produce in the body are concerned.

The first large group of emotions includes those whose changes consist in *overstimulation* of various parts of the body: an overstimulation, via the nervous system, of any organ or any muscle; overstimulation of one or more of the endocrine glands.

Because these emotions overstimulate organs and muscles, they produce a feeling that is unpleasant. People for thousands of years have naturally called these the "unpleasant emotions." These include such well-known ones as anger, anxiety, fear, apprehension, discouragement, grief, and dissatisfaction. Actually, there is no limit to the variety and nuance of emotions; one could make a list of unpleasant emotions a mile long.

The second large group of emotions are those whose manifestations in the body are an *optimal stimulation,* one neither too extreme nor too weak. These are the emotions that we can lump together under the long-used term of "pleasant emotions." We call them pleasant because the changes they produce give us a pleasant feeling. These are the emotions like hope, joy, courage, equanimity, affection, and agreeableness. Here again the possible list is endless; there is no limit to their variety.

➡ Some of the Manifestations of the Emotion of Anger

Let us see what the actual manifestations of a specific emotion are. We will take an emotion that you and I, of course, have never had, but that we have seen other people have — the emotion of *anger.*

In any emotion, there are external manifestations — that is, changes one can see exhibited externally on the surface of the body. These external manifestations make acting possible, for acting consists in duplicating the external manifestations of as many emotions as possible. A good actor can command many more than a poor actor. We can tell simply by looking at him whether he is portraying happiness, dissatisfaction, fear, and so on.

The manifestations of the emotion of anger are so numerous that Dr. W. B. Cannon, of Harvard University, who studied them in detail, required an entire printed page to merely list them.

The chief external manifestations in the emotion of anger are: a reddening of the skin of the face, a widening of the eyelids, bloodshot whites of the eyes, contraction and tightening of the lips, a setting of the jaw, clenching of the fists, a tremor in the arms, and very often a tremor in the voice. You know immediately on seeing anyone with such manifestations that he is in a state of anger.

But the internal manifestations, that is, the changes that are occurring inside the body, are much more profound and remarkable. For example, when you become angry, your blood immediately clots quicker than normal — not just a little quicker, but a whole lot quicker. An emotion is a very fundamental biological change and most of the manifestations are of some biological significance. Obviously, the blood-clotting change in anger serves a biological purpose. In the emotion of anger one is very apt to have a fight, to receive a wound, and to bleed; it is then beneficial to have the blood clot quickly.

Another similar biologically valuable manifestation is that the moment you become angry the number of blood cells in the circulating blood increases by as much as a half a million per cubic millimeter. When a person becomes angry, the muscles at the outlet of the stomach squeeze down so tightly that nothing leaves the stomach during anger, and the entire digestive tract becomes so spastic that many people have severe abdominal pains either during or after a fit of anger.

The heart rate goes up markedly during anger, often to 180 or 220, or higher, and stays there until the anger has passed. The blood pressure rises markedly and steeply from a normal of 130 or so to 230 or more. This is a manifestation that often produces dire results. You have possibly known of a person who developed a stroke during a fit of anger because his blood pressure rose so high he "blew" a blood vessel in his brain.

Also, in anger, the coronary arteries in the heart squeeze down, hard enough to produce angina pectoris, or even a fatal coronary occlusion. This happens fairly frequently.

John Hunter, one of the greatest physiologists England ever had, had the uncomfortable combination of a ready temper and a bad set of coronary arteries. Hunter always said that the first rascal who really got him mad would kill him. His wife came close to finishing him a couple of times, but the rascal finally appeared at a medical meeting and made him so angry he dropped dead of a coronary occlusion.

You can readily see how, if a man were angry enough of the time, the manifestations of his emotions might produce physical symptoms — such as abdominal pain, exhausted heart, apoplexy, or a coronary occlusion.

Fortunately there are not very many men who are angry continually, although there are some. But we do find people, and many of them, who have some of the other unpleasant emotions continually.

➧ Examples of Single Emotions Producing Single Symptoms

Let me give you two further examples (that you have doubtless seen yourself) of how a single emotion can produce a single symptom.

You have seen, or heard of, a person who faints when he looks at blood. He doesn't faint because he has a weak heart or a high blood pressure. He faints because the sight of blood produces the emotion of fear, and part of the manifestation of the emotion of fear is a squeezing down of some of the blood vessels supplying the brain — this produces the faint.

In other people, the sight of blood may cause vomiting, not because they have a disease of the stomach, but because, in them, the sight of blood produces the emotion of disgust. Part of the manifestation of the emotion of disgust is a contraction of the stomach violent enough to cause vomiting.

➧ A Single Violent Emotion May Cause Sudden, Severe Illness

Occasionally, a severe emotionally induced illness may follow one single severe emotion

A man was carried into our clinic one morning at nine o'clock. He was carried in because he couldn't possibly have walked; he was too weak and too dizzy to stand. His heart was going 180 beats a minute. He was vomiting. He couldn't control his bowels; he couldn't control his urine. He stayed in that condition in the hospital for three months, during which time there were moments when we thought he couldn't live any longer.

Until eight o'clock that morning, this man had been a perfectly healthy and unusually strong man. At about eight o'clock, he walked into his wife's bedroom and discovered that his wife had killed their only daughter and then committed suicide. From the time he made that discovery, he was a very sick man. It was not that he had acquired cancer, or tuberculosis, or heart trouble, although he was as ill as though he had developed all three. What he had developed was powerfully unpleasant emotions.

Let's not forget this: Any one of the rest of us, with that man's mental background, in that man's situation, would have developed the same sort of violent illness. No one is immune to emotionally induced illness.

➤ Most E. I. I. Comes from Relatively Small, Unpleasant Emotions

Most of the emotionally induced illness we physicians see in our offices does not come as the result of one large, terrific emotion, nor even from any series of catastrophes. Instead, most cases of emotionally induced illness are the result of a monotonous drip, drip of seemingly unimportant yet nevertheless unpleasant emotions, the everyday run of anxieties, fears, discouragements and longings. Clinically, we've known this to be true for years. But a peculiar thing in medicine is that we never believe anything unless it can be demonstrated in animals.

Monotonous repetition of unpleasant emotions. A few years ago two Cornell psychologists, H. S. Liddell and A. V.

Moore, demonstrated that the monotonous repetition of rather minor unpleasant emotions can produce E. E. I., at least in sheep.[1]

These two investigators tied a light wire around one of the legs of one of the sheep, a wire so light that the sheep could carry it all about the field. At the end of a week of such wire pulling, the sheep was perfectly healthy and normal in every way.

For the next week, small electric shocks were sent through the wire; not hard shocks, just light shocks, so that the sheep twitched its leg slightly with each shock. Drs. Liddell and Moore could repeat this light shock as often as they pleased during the week. The sheep went right on eating in a perfectly normal fashion.

Then the two investigators tried varying the stimuli and they finally found that by introducing two other elements into the light shocks, they could produce a severe illness in any sheep in the field.

The first element was the introduction of *apprehension* into the shocks. This they did by ringing a bell ten seconds before they gave the shock. It was the same shock as before, not a bit stronger, but now when the sheep heard the bell, it stopped eating, or whatever it was doing, and waited apprehensively for the shock it soon learned was coming. But this new element alone was not enough to produce the disease.

The second element was monotonous repetition of the bell-shock apprehension. The interval of repetition did not make much difference as long as it was monotonously repeated. With this kind of treatment, every sheep it was tried upon soon showed signs of illness. It would first quit eating. Then it would stop following its companions around the field. Next it quit walking. Then it failed to stay on its feet. Finally it began to have difficulty in breathing. Then the experiment had to be stopped or the sheep would have died.

---

[1] H. S. Liddell, *The Neurotic Animals of Ithaca, N.Y. Science Illustrated,* February, 1949; 4:2, p. 26.

Once the monotonous repetition of apprehension was stopped, the sheep soon returned to normal.

The effect of interrupting monotonous apprehension. A most interesting and important secondary finding made by Drs. Liddell and Moore in their experiments on the sheep was that if the monotonous repetition of apprehension was interrupted for a period of two hours in every 24, none of the sheep would develop functional illness. A rest period less than two hours was ineffective.

It is thus apparent that to get E. I. I., the monotonous repetition of unpleasant emotions must be almost constant. To interrupt the stream completely each day would effec-tively prevent the disease. However, we do meet exceptional cases where an emotionally induced illness arises from a single precipitating event; these are always interesting and valuable in understanding and appreciating the profound nature of the illness. In addition to the case of the man whose wife committed suicide, another interesting example comes to mind.

The superintendent of schools in a neighboring city was a level-headed, well-adjusted individual who seemed as little likely to develop emotionally induced illness as anyone you could name. Then one day he developed a severe dizziness that could be relieved only by lying down. Just as soon as he attempted to sit upright, he became intensely dizzy and had to vomit. He was taken home and put to bed. There he stayed for many days, not improving. Nothing his physician gave him made him the least bit better. Then one day, as if by magic, he was better, and returned to school.

Some days afterward he went to his physician and said, "I wouldn't have thought that I could have emotions that would make me sick, but I am absolutely certain the illness I had was caused by a distressing series of emotions."

"What makes you say that?" asked his doctor.

"Some time ago, one of my best friends in this city asked me to back him up on a loan of a considerable sum of money.

It was such a large loan that I hesitated signing his note, since I knew that if the man failed to pay the note it would completely wipe me out of house and savings. Yet it seemed safe enough, and since the man was a good friend, I could not refuse. So I signed.

"It wasn't long after that the man was seriously hurt in an accident and spent months in the hospital, during which time it looked more and more as though his business venture was going to the wall. Worrying about that brought on my dizziness."

"But how can you be sure about that?" asked the doctor.

"Well, sir," went on the superintendent, "when I was in bed, feeling my sickest, this friend of mine for whom I had signed the note came to visit me, and told me that he had just been over to the bank and had paid off the note in full. From that moment, I started to recover. The next day I went back to school."

➡ *The Production of Symptoms in Emotionally Induced Illness*

Emotions manifest themselves through two different systems in the body. Some of the manifestations are mediated through the nervous system, others through the endocrine glands. Some of the symptoms can be produced *either* by way of the nervous system or by way of the endocrine system.

CHAPTER I IN A NUTSHELL

When you, or I, or any one of us, has a physical illness, the chances are better than 50 per cent that our illness is emotionally induced.

Emotionally induced illness is a *physical*, not a *mental* disease. It produces thousands of symptoms, varying from such homely ones as "pain in the neck" and "gas," to such complicated ones as "nephrosclerosis" and "peptic ulcer."

An emotion consists of chemical and physical changes *in the body* (either on the face, where they may be seen by others, or internally, where they are felt by us) — changes that are the *feeling* of every thought we think.

In the emotion of *anger*, the physical changes on the face *spell* anger. One of the internal changes in anger is an increase of blood pressure that sometimes breaks a cerebral blood vessel and produces a stroke. Another internal change that takes place in anger is a narrowing of the coronary blood vessels of the heart. This sometimes produces a coronary death.

The so-called "unpleasant" emotions are the ones whose internal changes produce the symptoms of disease.

The "pleasant" emotions produce changes that make us feel *good;* that is to say, they are optimal changes.

The chemical and physical changes in the body, which *are* the emotions, are mediated from the brain through the (1) autonomic nervous system, and through the (2) endocrine glands.

2. HOW YOUR EMOTIONS PRODUCE ILLNESS THROUGH YOUR NERVOUS SYSTEM

➡ The Manifestations of Emotions Mediated Through The Nervous System

The portion of the nervous system concerned with the emotions is the part called the *autonomic nervous system.* It is outside the control of the will. The brain center of the autonomic nervous system is the *hypothalamus,* which is also the center for pituitary gland stimulation. We shall see later that the pituitary gland is a more powerful agent for manifesting emotions than even the autonomic nervous system.

➡ Muscle Tension and the Production of Pain

Tense muscles are one of the most common sources of the general aches and pains we experience more or less constantly. The intense pain produced by a cramp illustrates very well how very severe muscle pains can be. If you will make a fist of your hand, not tightly, but firmly, you will find that it produces no pain at first. After a while, however, the muscle tension involved in making a fist begins to hurt more and more intensely.

The unpleasant emotions are commonly manifested by tightness both in the skeletal muscles and the muscles of the internal organs. If these muscle-tensing emotions are continued long enough, or if they are monotonously repeated, the muscles involved begin to hurt.

➤ *"So-and-so Gives Me a Pain in the Neck"*

The muscle groups most commonly involved in emotional manifestation are the muscles most commonly used. The muscles at the back of the neck, which are used more than any other set of skeletal muscles, are such a group. These same neck muscles are common sites of tense emotional manifestation. Eighty-five per cent of the patients complaining of a pain in the back of the head, radiating down the neck, have their pain as a result of *emotional* tightness in these muscles. This tension origin of neck pain was recognized years ago by that wise practical physiologist who first remarked that "So-and-so gives me a pain in the neck." Such a statement is literally true.

To demonstrate to yourself how emotions can tighten the muscles at the back of the neck, seat yourself in an easy chair tonight, and then worry hard about something for an hour. When you get up you will twist and stretch your neck because it feels tight, and the chances are that it will hurt.

➤ *The Common Lump in the Throat*

Another folk-saying is "I was so scared that my heart came up into my throat."

More commonly, patients complain of a lump in the throat. All the while, naturally, they are afraid they have some sort of a growth. Actually what 95 per cent of these patients have is an emotional tightness of the muscles at the upper end of the esophagus; this tightness feels like a lump. If the individual tries to swallow when these muscles are tight, there is a moment's hesitancy before the muscles loosen up, and the person feels as though he is choking. Then he becomes doubly sure there is something dreadfully wrong in his throat, and the lump becomes twice as bothersome.

➧ Cardiospasm, or Emotional Tightness of the Lower End of the Esophagus

The muscles at the lower end of the esophagus enter into emotional manifestation much less commonly than do the muscles at the upper end, and fortunately so. For when the lower esophageal muscles squeeze down, they are apt to stay "squoze" for days or even weeks, during which time nothing will run into the stomach, not even water. Such an individual would slowly starve if something were not done for him.

➧ Emotional Manifestation in the Muscles of the Stomach

The stomach is one of the organs *par excellence* for the manifestation of emotions. The emotional activities of the stomach are felt by everyone every day. When our worlds are going along well, we have a good appetite because the stomach is manifesting pleasant emotions. However, when things do not go well, we suddenly find that we have entirely lost our appetites. If then something good should happen, if an unknown uncle should leave us a cool million (whoopee) right away our appetite is back.

When the muscles of our stomachs tighten because of a certain variety of emotions, the resulting feeling is that of a lump in our upper abdomen; some people describe it as a "stone."

When the stomach muscles squeeze down *really hard,* a pain is produced, sometimes a very severe one. This pain often bears a considerable resemblance to the pain produced by an ulcer. We will see, in the next chapter, how ulcers are produced by the emotions, but we are speaking now of a muscle pain, not an ulcer pain.

Fully 50 per cent of the patients who complain of an ulcer-like pain are found not to have an ulcer but merely an emotional muscle pain of the stomach.

That the two pains resemble one another can be understood when one knows that even if one *has* an ulcer, it is not the ulcer that hurts, but the contraction of muscles next to the ulcer. A painfully-contracting muscle will feel the same whether an ulcer or an emotion is producing the spasm.

Some time ago I had as a patient a grocer who had an emotionally induced pain in his stomach. Being in competition with chain stores is a source of trouble sufficient to give one an emotional stomach pain. But that wasn't all the trouble this poor fellow had. I am sure that if I had had the man's wife, I would have had all his pain. And even that wasn't all — he also had a son who was always getting into trouble; not just a little trouble, but a whole lot of trouble. And between his grocery, his wife, and his son, this poor grocer had a pain in his stomach most of the time. And, of course, every once in a while some consultant would tell him that he had an ulcer. Then the thing really hurt. Whenever he went to doctors who knew what they were talking about, he was told that he had no ulcer. That didn't help his pain much because he was only made more confused, and that gave him pain.

But finally he began to believe that he had no ulcer. Every time he went to Northern Wisconsin for fishing, which he did twice a year, all he had to do was to get to Belleville, a town 25 miles north of his home, and there, on the main street of Belleville, his pain stopped. It did not return again until two weeks later when, on his way home, he came to Round Grove Hill and caught sight of the courthouse tower in his home town. There his pain started again.

At the Mayo Clinic, there used to be a famous doctor who had the same kind of pain. He knew what his pain was, but he said that as long as he was in Rochester with patients pushing and pulling him, and with many things on his mind, he would have his pain almost all the time. To get rid of the pain all he had to do was to get on the train, and when the train came to Winona — no, when the train came to the center of the bridge crossing the Mississippi — the pain left, not to return until the train again pulled into the Rochester station and he looked out to see the Clinic tower.

The doctor's analysis of why the pain left in the center of the bridge was this: that was where the train left Minnesota, and he never had liked Minnesota.

My grocer patient said that he had always admired Belleville — in fact, he had always wanted to live there — and when he reached its main street, he had a feeling of well-being for the first time in weeks. That was where his pain stopped.

➤ *The Colon Is the Mirror of the Mind*

The same kind of painful spasm can occur, and does occur, in the 28 feet of intestine that lie beyond the stomach, but most especially in the part known as the colon. The colon, *more than any other organ*, is a manifestor of the emotions. So much so that a wise doctor in Philadelphia remarked some years ago that "the colon is the mirror of the mind, and when the mind gets tight, the colon gets tight."

One of the most remarkable things about emotional manifestation is illustrated by the colon, and I wish to call your attention to it here. In any given individual the same emotion will be manifested in the same way every time it occurs. If, in one individual, the muscles at the back of the neck squeeze down every time he gets anxious, these same muscles will always act the same with the same emotion.

In some other individual it may be a three-inch segment of the colon that squeezes down hard with a similar emotion, and it will always be the same three-inch segment that responds to the emotion.

If this spasm happens to be in the colon in the upper right-hand portion of the abdomen, it will produce a pain very similar to a gallstone colic. Fifty per cent of the people we see with fairly typical "gall bladder attacks" turn out to have normal gall bladders. They are having their attacks from emotional spasm of their colon, or some other adjacent muscle. Dr. Andrew C. Ivy, Chicago physiologist, showed that an emotional spasm of the small sphincter muscle at the bile duct outlet can also produce a pain as severe as any gall bladder attack.

➤ Emotionally Induced Gall-Bladder-Like Pain

Probably every doctor has at some time mistaken an emotional colon spasm for a gall bladder attack. I admit I have. I was called to see a patient who had all the symptoms and findings of a very severe gall-bladder colic. Any other doctor seeing her that day would have made the same diagnosis. I had to give her three "hypos" before the pain finally abated. I paid too little attention to the fact that the patient's only son had received notice of the draft only two days before.

Two days after her son had left for an army camp, the lady had a second and similar attack, which again had all the earmarks of gall bladder disease. Again, three "hypos."

The third and most severe attack occurred three months later, two days after the patient had received word that her son had left New York City for overseas, destination not announced. On that occasion, the patient was so very ill that I had to move her to the hospital. When gall bladder X-rays were taken, I was surprised to find a normal gall bladder. Nevertheless, I felt so certain that the gall bladder contained stones invisible to X-rays, that I advised operative removal of the gall bladder. This the patient agreed to, and the gall bladder was removed.

Following this, the patient did well for many months. I was about ready to regard myself as a remarkably clever fellow when the lady had her fourth severe attack of right-upper-quadrant pain, this time without benefit of the gall bladder. This attack occurred two days after she had received word that her son had landed in North Africa, and the papers carried the news that fighting had started with the Germans. A fifth attack occurred when she learned that her son had been wounded. Following this, the boy returned home and the lady has had no spells since.

➡ Emotional "Appendicitis"

If the emotional spasm of the colon occurs in the right lower quadrant of the abdomen, it will look for all the world like an attack of appendicitis. Even a very smart doctor may be unable to make a positive diagnosis, especially in children in whom this kind of thing is especially apt to occur. Very often, to be safe, the surgeon will open the abdomen, only to find a normal appendix and a bowel squeezed down so tight that it is blanched white.

In other people, painful spasms may occur throughout the entire length of the colon, and believe me, these people are intensely uncomfortable.

There are so many emotional disturbances of the colon that all sort of terms have been evolved for them like "spastic colon," "irritable colon," "nonspecific ulcerative colitis," and many other terms, all of them merely synonyms for "emotional colon."

➡ "Gas"

One of the commonest complaints people have is of "gas" and "bloating." "Doctor," they will say, "everything I eat goes to gas." "Doctor, I bloat up something terrible," or, "When this gas forms, it crowds my heart." One patient even said that her gas, which "came from her food, went up through her chest, through her neck and whistled out through her ear."

It always surprises these patients, as it did me when I first heard it, to hear that not even a little bit of gas is formed in the process of our digestion. All the gas that we get in our stomachs and intestines is swallowed when we eat our food or swallow our saliva.

The thing that is happening when we have "gas," or "bloating," is that one or more of the three-inch segments of the small bowel is squeezing down tightly. These spasms are so tight that they produce temporary obstructions through which nothing can pass. These spastic obstructions may last from five to 60 minutes, or even longer. The liquid and gaseous content of the intestine is carried up against this obstruction by the normal peristalsis of the bowel, and the intestine, consequently, balloons up. The victim feels this ballooning, or bloating, along with the spasm, as a very disagreeable feeling. When the spasm is finally rather suddenly relieved, the contents of the ballooned bowel shoots ahead with an angry gurgle which one can feel and often hear. With this relief of pressure the individual says to himself, "There goes my gas."

That, my dyspeptic friend, is what gas is. Under the X-ray fluoroscope, I have viewed as many as 18 or 20 such spasms occurring at the same time in the same person. Believe me, he was an uncomfortable human, *and he wasn't imagining it.*

To our patients suffering with "gas," we show colored photographs of an opened abdomen on an operating table. The patient photographed was a young man with a considerable police record. For certain medical reasons, his abdominal operation was performed under local anesthesia so that only his abdominal wall was anesthetized. When the abdomen had been opened, the small intestines and colon were in full view and appeared normal.

The first picture was made. Then the surgeon said to the patient, "Have you had any encounters with the police lately?" knowing full well that the police were waiting for the fellow at the front door as soon as he was dismissed from the hospital. Within a minute, several visible spasms formed in the small bowel with typical ballooning behind the spasm.

Then the second picture was taken. The surgeon asked, "How do you feel now?" The young man answered, "I'm all bloated."

➡ From the Emotions, Too, Stem Most Belches

Belching is very much the same thing, except that it occurs in the stomach. I don't, of course, mean the lusty animal belch that escapes after a big meal or a glass of beer, but the more embarrassing belching you see many people struggle with whenever they become disturbed or under pressure. I know a very good public speaker, who, during his first ten minutes of feeling out his audience, struggles with himself, often unsuccessfully, to hold down the belches. Once he finds himself and hits his stride, he leaves his belches behind.

I'll never forget a patient I saw in 1942. The poor miserable man was belching at a constant rate of once every 30 seconds! He did this whether he was at home, at church, or in my office. And it had been going on for a week. Believe me, he wanted to get rid of it! Nothing he had tried had helped in the least. One surgeon had advised cutting the phrenic nerves to immobilize the diaphragm.

Here is how his belching started: In the spring of 1942, he had sold his farm and bought a bakery, a business entirely new to him. In 1942, you will remember, sugar, flour, lard, all the ingredients he needed in his bakery, were strictly rationed. The poor chap was as poor at arithmetic as he was at the bakery business, and very soon he was in such difficulties with the local rationing board that the Federal agents were being called in. Just at this time his consternation became abysmal because his baker, on whom he absolutely depended, was called by the draft. The poor owner started to do what you and I would probably also have done under the circumstances — he started to belch.

There was obviously only one treatment. That was to sell his bakery and get out. When this was suggested, the poor man smiled for the first time in our acquaintance. Twelve hours after the sale was consummated, the man quit belching, to his infinite relief.

➤ Be Choosy, if You Must Have Bad Emotions

You see what problems the emotions that manifest themselves in the digestive tract can produce. If you must have them, therefore, try to pick out an emotion which manifests itself in the left side of your colon; there are fewer emergency operations possible on that side.

➤ Emotional Manifestations in the Muscles of the Blood Vessels

So far we have dealt with symptoms produced by emotional manifestation in the muscles of the digestive tract. But all the other muscles of the body are influenced by the emotions, especially the muscles that are to be found in the walls of all but the very smallest blood vessels. One of the more obvious and common emotional responses of the blood vessels is blushing. But there are many others.

The moderate-sized blood vessels, lying inside or outside the skull, are highly sensitive to emotional stimuli. As these vessels contract, emotionally, headache is produced, both the common type of headache, or the more severe type we know as migraine. Fully 85 per cent of all headaches are emotionally induced. In some individuals the causal connection between the emotional disturbance and the headache is clearly evident. But sometimes it is not so apparent.

The emotional excitant may be some deeply-seated trouble which the person may try to hide even from himself, one he certainly would not tell anyone else even if he could. But the emotions behind most headaches are easy enough to spot.

For example, one of my patients developed a terrific migraine, that kept her in bed for a day, every time she went to town. She was a fastidious housekeeper, living on a farm. Going to town meant getting her house in spic-and-span condition, getting the children cleaned and dressed, thinking of what she had to do in town, and becoming apprehensive about meeting people, because she was very shy. By the time she started for town, her headache had started, and when she returned home, she would have to go to bed. The cure for her headaches was obvious — not to go to town. She does, of course, occasionally — sometimes it is to see her doctor. She goes home with her headache.

Emotionally induced skin trouble. But blood vessels manifesting emotions can do even more remarkable things. Fully 30 per cent of the skin trouble in these United States is what the dermatologists call *neurodermatitis.* A neurodermatitis can occur anywhere on the body. In the skin involved, the small blood vessels in the second layer are constantly squeezing down in emotional manifestation. Every time they do so a small amount of serum is extruded through the thin layer of the vessel. As this continues, an appreciable amount of serum accumulates in the tissues. First, the skin gets slightly brawny, then red. Soon there is enough serum under pressure to force its way to the surface, and one has the weeping, scaling, crusting, and itching of a full-blown case of neurodermatitis.

One of my patients was a man of 73 with a terrific generalized neurodermatitis, which he had had for some years. He had never had any skin disease until he was 68. At 67, his first wife died, and at 68, he married his second wife, a lady of his own age. It was on their honeymoon that he first developed his dermatitis, and when they got home, it was so severe that he soon had to be hospitalized. After a week in the hospital, the skin would be very much better and he would return home, only to have the whole thing recur a short time later.

In the course of time he had to go to a town several hundred miles away on business. After being there a week, his neurodermatitis cleared up. The next time it became bad again at home, he returned to Moline because it was cheaper than going to the hospital. Some time later he went to another distant town on business, and found that there, too, his dermatitis cleared up in a week. Finally, his wife had to leave home to care for a sick relative, and our patient stayed home alone, and lo and behold, after a week, his skin was clear. The connection had become obvious enough.

We asked him, "What did you discover about your wife during your honeymoon?" He had the answer ready immediately: "I found out that she was domineering and dominating, and I just can't stand it!" We then took his wife aside and explained to her that she was causing her husband's dermatitis. She didn't like to believe it, but she promised that she would lean over backwards trying not to be domineering. She performed admirably, and the man's neurodermatitis left completely. Occasionally, there is a hint of return, and then we simply talk to the wife once more.

➤ Emotional Manifestation in Skeletal Muscles

We saw earlier in this chapter how tightening of the neck muscles caused our most common neck pain.

It was learned by careful study during World War II that the thing we have called *muscular rheumatism,* or *myofibrositis,* or *fibrositis,* is almost invariably produced by emotional tension. During the first World War, a certain percentage of the boys in the trenches developed fibrositis. It was thought to be due to the wet, miserable, and exposed living conditions in the trenches. But in the second World War, almost exactly the same percentage of the boys in the battle line developed fibrositis. The percentage was the same whether they were fighting in the cold, wet Aleutian Islands, or in hot, dry North Africa.

It was found, furthermore, that the incidence of fibrositis increased steadily as the boys moved forward from the base camps toward the fighting front. And it was eventually determined that an emotion was responsible — the emotion a person has when he is called upon to do something he would not do if compulsion were not upon him.

In this situation he involuntarily steels himself and tightens certain muscles — very often those of the shoulder girdle. This also occurs, of course, in individuals in civilian life who must constantly meet situations they would rather avoid. If such situations are acute enough, or if they are of long enough duration, pain is eventually produced.

One of the common sites of such pain is the pectoral muscle of the left chest. The same thing, of course, can occur in the pectoral muscle of the right chest. But a person pays much more attention to a pain in the left chest than one in the right, and becomes much more alarmed, because he fears, more and more, as the pain goes on, that he has heart disease. All he needs then is for some uncertain doctor to murmur that "You might have a little heart trouble," and he is off on a long emotionally induced and physician-augmented illness.

Fibrositis is an exceedingly common cause of pain in human beings. Most people will get a fibrositis at some time or other, and *some* people are subject to fibrositis all the time. I happen to be one of the latter; I have a fibrositis most of the time. And, of course, it is emotionally induced. Every day I am compelled to see more people in my office than a doctor ought to see — so many, that seeing them thoroughly constitutes severe physical and emotional pressure. So I am hurting somewhere most of the time, especially if the irate relatives of a particularly sick patient camp on my trail.

When I leave on a vacation, my fibrositis stays behind in my office; when I get back to my office, I put it on again. Right now, for instance, I have a fibrositis in my right shoulder area so severe that I can't push a screen door open. The important thing is that I recognize properly what my pain is, and what its source is. Then I don't worry about it.

Many other people, who do not have the fortune to be doctors, worry about their fibrositis. They fear, perhaps, they are filled to the brim with cancer, or they believe they have crippling rheumatism, and apprehensively expect to be crippled and incapacitated. Nothing could be further from the truth.

Fibrositis never becomes crippling; it becomes incapacitating only if you let it. It is not serious; it merely belongs in the class of confounded nuisances.

➤ Most of Us Hurt Somewhere Almost All the Time

I must deviate here just a moment to call attention to a very important point that, when it is unrealized, is apt to start many people on the long, hard road of bellyaching.

If at any time on a busy day we stop and ask ourselves, "Where do I hurt?" we can usually find a pain somewhere, perhaps in a foot, perhaps in the lower abdomen. Sometimes, out of nowhere, there will come a very severe momentary pain: perhaps in the thigh, perhaps in the chest, a pain severe enough to make us pause a moment in our hectic flight. Such pains are part of the normal processes of living. For no explainable reason, a pain-nerve-ending is being stimulated, or a blood vessel is contracting painfully, or a muscle bundle is cramping. Some people feel these pains more readily than others because their threshold to pain sensations is lower than other people's.

The late Dr. E. Libman, of New York City, one of America's great physicians, some years ago, called attention to the fact that some people are more susceptible to pain than other people, not because they are bigger babies, but simply because they feel pain more readily. He devised a simple clinical test to tell how sensitive to pain a person is. It consists in pressing against the *styloid process*, which lies just below the lobe of the ear, behind the angle of the jaw. A non-sensitive person will not wince when the styloid process is pressed, whereas a person who is sensitive to pain will draw away and make an awful grimace.

A person who is very sensitive to pain *will feel the normal*

peristaltic contractions of his intestines as a pain. I am italiciz-
ing that sentence because it explains why some people have
a *continual* discomfort or pain in their abdomens. Unless
they appreciate their sensitiveness to pain, and realize the
cause of their abdominal pain, these people will be chronically ill all their lives, and the victims of all the organically-
minded physicians in the country.

Anyone feeling one of the common pains all of us experience every day can work it up into quite a major experience
if he puts all his attention and awareness into it. To make
such a minimal pain worse, all one needs to do is to center
one's awareness upon it. It will begin to perform for him,
growing bolder and more magnificent until it can be worked
up into quite a thing.

Another factor that will magnify and aggravate any minimal pain is the development of any tension state. It has been
shown in a number of different ways that an anxiety state
lowers the threshold of pain. Sensations that we would term
mildly painful, or that we would overlook altogether when
we are in a happy state, will become very painful at times
when we are emotionally distressed.

It is partly for this reason that so many people develop
low backaches when they are under emotional tension. Everyone experiences a low backache at some time or other.
Usually, after a bit of muscle strain, it may be so mild that
one pays no attention to it; but during emotional stress, the
threshold of pain becomes so lowered that the painful
stimuli in the back are highly magnified.

➡ *You Have Read Only a Very Partial List of Emotional Muscular Symptoms*

In this chapter, I have listed a few of the commoner and
the more interesting symptoms produced by emotional manifestation in the muscles. There are as many more as there are
muscles in the body and organs that contain muscles. It would

Fellowship for Today
Lending Library

You are preparing a permanent record for our library,
so please print or write legibly.

Title: _HOW TO LIVE 365 DAYS A YEAR_

Author: _JOHN SCHINDLER_

☑ book   ☐ audio cassette   ☐ videotape

☐ other (please specify): _____

This item is a: ☐ gift   ☑ loan

PT

Given by: _DEE BRAKER_

on _5/17/97_   (name)

(date)

be too time-consuming and too boring for you if I listed them all.

I simply wish to give you an idea of how our emotions, *your* emotions, work to produce illness.

If we realize that this is true, that it is true in ourselves, then we do not need to feel apprehensive over most of the discomforts we feel in ourselves. By realizing this, we will have made the first great step (and the most important one) in avoiding the disease that is causing more morbidity, more disability, more misery, more absenteeism, and more accidents than all the other diseases this human clay can contract.

Certainly this is important, primarily important, to every one of us.

BRIEF SUMMARY OF CHAPTER 2

The emotional effects produced through the autonomic nervous system are less severe than those produced through the endocrine glands, but they are more common and just as disagreeable. A common nerve effect is a tight muscle; a tight muscle is painful, whether it is in a leg, in a blood vessel wall, or in the stomach.

Thus emotionally tight muscles produce pain in the back of the neck, in the stomach, in the colon, in the scalp, in blood vessels, in skeletal muscles. Emotionally tight muscles produce ulcer-like pains, gall bladder-like pains, common headaches, migraine headaches, and a great host of clinical pictures. Another blood vessel effect is neurodermatitis, which constitutes 30 per cent of all skin disease.

The phenomenon that we ordinarily term "gas" is in reality an emotional spasm of muscles in the small intestines. Most belches are emotional muscle effects in the stomach.

3. HOW EMOTIONAL OVERBREATHING AFFECTS YOU

➡ *We All Hyperventilate at Times*

There is one set of symptoms, emotionally induced, that is especially common, and that produces severe apprehension in the people who experience it. This set of symptoms is known medically as *the hyperventilation syndrome*. It is of interest historically, since it was the first syndrome known to be emotionally induced in which a chemical factor plays a leading role.

The chance is that you too have experienced the hyperventilation syndrome at some time or other.

By *hyperventilation* we simply mean breathing too deeply, or too fast, or both. You have noticed that if you become acutely disturbed, you will breathe faster than usual. Actors, whose art consists mainly in portraying the external manifestations of emotions, do the same on the stage. Normally, most of us breathe between 16 and 18 times a minute at rest. If we were to increase our rate to 22 or 23 times a minute, we ourselves, or those near us, would probably not notice the difference, but our bodies would soon notice the increase, in ways we will describe in a moment.

➤ *What Happens When You Hyperventilate*

When we breathe faster than normal, more carbon dioxide is being lost from the blood through the lungs than is being formed in the body. Consequently, the level of carbon dioxide in the blood gradually drops to a point at which things begin to happen.

About the first thing that happens is a crawling sensation under the skin. Next, there is a perceptible numbness of the fingers, hands, and other parts of the body, gradually becoming more pronounced, until finally there is a sensation of needles pricking the skin all over. But long before the numbness becomes as acute as that, other symptoms appear. The heart starts to race; there is a trembling feeling, at first inside, and later all over the body. Lightheadedness, or even fainting, occurs. Finally, cramps appear increasingly hard until it seems that every skeletal muscle is cramping; the legs and arms draw up in a painful spastic position known as *tetany*. We have patients who, when they are upset, will go through the entire gamut of hyperventilation and end up in tetany.

A farmer, for instance, called up excitedly one day because his son had just fallen out of the haymow. I hurried out to his farm, and, on arriving there, I found the father lying on the floor in tetany, because he had hyperventilated so hard in his excitement. He needed attention more than did the son who had fallen out of the haymow. This man had these hyperventilation episodes ever so often.

One day a dentist in town called me to come immediately to his office because this same farmer was having (the dentist said) a fit. But I found him lying on the floor in tetany. He had been so apprehensive all day about going to the dentist that he had been hyperventilating. The pay-off came in the dentist's chair.

In other patients, some of the other symptoms of hyperventilation stand out more prominently than the cramps. It is quite common to find a terrified patient with the sensation of a thousand needles all over him, and his heart beating wildly. He is naturally terrified, because if he ever felt as though he were going to die, it is at that moment. Other patients will become very lightheaded, or may faint, during or after hyperventilation. One young lady had not been able to get out of bed for two months because she hyperventilated so constantly that she fainted as soon as she tried to stand.

➡ *Hyperventilation Is Common During Sleep*

One of the most interesting things about hyperventilation is that it occurs most commonly in our sleep. If you will watch a sleeping person, especially someone who is in a troublesome life situation, you will see him breathe more rapidly and deeply for a time, and then lapse into quiet breathing, only to repeat the whole cycle over again.

Our minds are never at rest; we are dreaming every minute of the night; and at night in our sleep, the usual censor — common sense — is not around.

If someone on our street says something nasty to disturb us during the day, at night in our dreams that person, at the head of a band of Indians, is probably chasing us toward a precipitous cliff. In our sleep, we react emotionally as though we really were being driven toward catastrophe. We roll and toss — and we hyperventilate.

About once every week during my 20 years of medical practice, I have had to see someone about 2:00 A. M. who awoke during hyperventilation — probably just at the point where he was about to be hurled over the cliff. When he awakens, the stage of hyperventilation is usually at the point where his heart is racing and his hands are numb. Naturally, he thinks he is dying of heart trouble. One such call came from a distance of 15 miles. The husband yelled into the phone, "My wife is dying of a heart attack. Come quick!"

I knew them both, and I would have given odds of ten to

one that she was hyperventilating. When I arrived I was glad I had gone, because both husband and wife had hyperventilated to the point of tetany, and needed medical relief in the worst sort of way.

This is what had happened: The wife had awakened from sleep to find her hands numb and her heart beating wildly. Her first thought was, "I am having a stroke like my mother had." She awakened her husband and told him how she felt. His first thought was, "My wife is having a heart attack like my father had." They then both got more excited, and continued to hyperventilate. To their surprise, they lived.

At other times a person may not awaken until hyperventilation has produced cramps in the legs. This is a common cause of leg cramps at night, a condition which can be prevented rather simply by an inexpensive pill.

THE GIST OF CHAPTER 3

A person under stress is likely to hyperventilate, that is, breathe more rapidly than normal, without being aware of it. In doing so, he breathes out enough carbon dioxide to lower the level of carbon dioxide in the blood. As this blood level of carbon dioxide drops, the person experiences numbness, tingling, rapid heart action, internal quivering, fainting, weakness and cramps. He may experience all of them, or some more prominently than others.

Since hyperventilation is apt to occur with the emotions produced by the dreams in our sleep, we often awaken feeling some of the symptoms of hyperventilation, and, if we don't know what they are, we are apt to fear impending disaster.

4. HOW YOUR EMOTIONS PRODUCE DISEASE THROUGH YOUR GLANDS

❧ It's NOT Your Nerves

Doctors and people knew for a long time that the nervous system had, in some way, a great deal to do with emotionally induced illness. Remarks such as these are common:

"It's your nerves."

"I'm all nerves."

"If I could only do something about my nerves."

"My nerves are in a terrible condition."

"I'm just a bundle of nerves."

"If my nerves were only better."

Actually, there is nothing wrong with the nerves in E. I. I. They are just as organically normal as the rest of the body. All the nerves have to do with it is that they act as a messenger telling the colon to contract or telling the heart to speed up.

As I say, we've known for a long time that the nervous system was in some vague sort of way tied up in E. I. I. Then doctors like Lange, Cannon, Dunbar, Wolf, and Wolff, and many others began to show us more precisely just how the thing works. We reviewed a few of these mechanisms that are mediated by the nervous system in the last two chapters.

Dr. Hans Selye. Then along came Dr. Hans Selye of Montreal.[1] He started his work as recently as 1936. Many others have joined him, or have followed the leads Dr. Selye pioneered. And today a tremendous and amazing new chapter — a new understanding — is being written on emotionally induced illness. The wildest things we imagined before 1936, or could have imagined about the mechanism of E. I. I. are a tame understatement compared to the things which have become known. And the accumulation of the new knowledge has barely started.

We do know today that the group of organs in the body we call the endocrine glands have as much to do with emotional manifestation as the nervous system has. What is more important, the endocrine effects of the emotions far outweigh the nerve effects in magnitude and importance. So much so that it would be closer to the truth to say, "It's my endocrines," rather than, "It's my nerves."

➡ The Pituitary Gland

Dr. Selye started with investigations of the pituitary gland. Merely from the pituitary gland's location in the most inaccessible part of the body, one might surmise that the pituitary gland must be of vital importance. Located inside the cranium, on the underside of the brain, the pituitary is nestled and cradled in a complete bowl of bone, protected against almost any conceivable injury. One might surmise, from this protected position, the pituitary is about the most important organ we have. And it is.

The pituitary is only about the size and shape of an over-

---

[1] An excellent summary of Dr. Hans Selye's monumental work can be found in his book, *The Story of the Adaptation Syndrome*, 1952, Acta, Montreal, Canada.

grown pea. Yet despite this insignificant size, the pituitary is the master regulator of the entire body. It produces an amazing variety of hormones (hormones are substances carried in the blood, which act on other parts of the body) some of which are known, one of which has been secured in *pure* form, and several others that are suspected but not yet demonstrated.

We know there is one hormone of the pituitary that raises blood pressure, another that makes smooth muscles contract, one that inhibits the kidneys from producing urine, one that stimulates the kidneys to make more urine. Then there is a whole group of hormones that regulate the other endocrine glands of the body. These other glands produce many more hormones to regulate just about everything that goes on in our bodies.

Your pituitary is always on the job. The pituitary is like a key industry that works quietly but efficiently night and day making certain commodities that are absolutely essential to the well-being of our body. The well-being of the entire body is dependent on its smooth operation.

But this factory — the pituitary — is more important than that. Not only does it control our physiology in time of peace and quiet, but it becomes the key defense plant if the body is threatened in any way, shape, or form. With *any kind* of a threat to the safety of the body, this key industry puts out the commodity necessary to mobilize the defenses against that threat.

Stress and stressors. These threats to the body Dr. Hans Selye called "stressors," and the action of a "stressor" a "stress." The pituitary reacts to a vast variety of stressors that threaten our well-being in any way. The pituitary is not only the master regulator of the body under normal conditions, but also the organ that adapts the body to meet threatening conditions.

Stressors that threaten the well-being of the body are extremely numerous. One stressor will stimulate the pituitary to produce one hormone in excess, or a combination of hormones in excess. Another stressor will stimulate the production of another hormone.

Two such stressors are bacterial invasion and virus infection, in response to which the pituitary puts out a hormone that mobilizes the body defenses. Other stressors are exposure to heat or to cold, exposure to excessive moisture or dryness, severe muscular exertion, drug effects, injuries, operations, and many others.

Dr. Selye learned from his experiments that the greatest stressors are the psychic stressors, the unpleasant emotions. The unpleasant emotions can stimulate any or all of the many hormones. *What is more, a very acute emotion will produce immediate, profound effects to a much greater degree than will any other type of stressor.*

Witness the man we told about, in chapter two, who became violently ill when his wife killed their only daughter and then took her own life. But, what is even more important, it is characteristic of emotional stress to act over a longer period of time than do the other stressors, often for months, or years, whereas the stress of an infection usually lasts only a week or two and exposure to physical effects of muscular overexertion even less long. We shall see in a moment how important this long-time effect is.

▶ *The Diuretic Hormone*

The *diuretic hormone* is relatively unimportant, but it illustrates how stressors, including emotional stress, act.

The diuretic hormone makes the kidneys excrete an increased amount of urine. I'm sure you remember having had somewhat the same experience with the diuretic hormone that a boy in our local school did the other day. The boy was about to take a final examination in geography, for which he felt himself utterly unprepared. He was tense, anxious, and apprehensive. Two minutes before the examination was about to start, the boy suddenly realized that he must, that he simply *must*, leave the room. He didn't merely imagine that he must, he really and truly had to.

His emotions had stimulated the pituitary to produce the diuretic hormone which, in turn, stimulated the kidneys to excrete an increased amount of urine. Not to have left the room would have ended in acute misery, and probably in disaster. Actually the latter happened, because the teacher was not wise in the ways of hormones and emotions, and refused to let him leave the room. The parents called me in as a sort of a medical-legal advisor. The upshot was that the boy was given credit for passing the geography exam that the accident prevented him from taking. The boy can thank his stars that there are emotions and hormones.

➤ *The Somatotrophic Hormone*

STH. One of the most important hormones made by the pituitary is the *somatotrophic hormone*, known for short as STH. STH acts directly on the body, but it also induces the adrenal glands to produce DOCA (desoxycorticosterone), which also acts like STH. STH mobilizes the body's defenses (antibodies, white blood cells, and so forth) against any kind of an infection. But in addition, STH, and not the bacteria, produces the picture we know simply as "being sick."

We used to think that the picture of "being sick" was directly due to the toxins of the bacteria or virus. Dr. Selye has shown beyond question that STH is responsible for our "being sick." *Any* infecting agent produces the same general initial picture.

If the infection is mild, as with a cold, or light flu, the picture of sickness is very mild — perhaps a headache, tiredness, loss of appetite, and an increase in temperature of a few tenths of a degree. But if the infection is more severe, the production of STH is greater, and the picture is much more severe. Locally, at the site of the infection, there is an inflammation with redness, swelling, and heat; the temperature may rapidly climb to 105°, as in pneumonia; there are general aches and pains, headaches, gastrointestinal upsets, loss of appetite, loss of weight, albumin in the urine, an increased elimination of nitrogen, potassium and phosphates, and often a skin rash. All these effects, and many more, are produced by STH. As we shall see later, they disappear very rapidly if one injects ACTH, which opposes STH.

But the main importance of STH is that it mobilizes the defenses of the body against infection at the same time that it produces the symptoms of being sick. It mobolizes the antibodies and the phagocytic cells. In fact, the symptoms of being sick are in themselves a defensive and beneficial reaction to an invading germ. If it were not for STH, we would die with the first cold.

STH is also stressed by dark, dismal, futile, despairing emotions. One will see patients like Mrs. G——, who, when she gets an ordinary cold that produces a mild STH stress, becomes morbidly despondent and despairing at the idea of having a cold. Consequently, she adds the emotional stress of STH to that of the infection. As a result, Mrs. G—— is always as sick with a very mild cold as she would be with a severe pneumonia. Actually her resistance to infection is superb because of the splendid STH output. But even after every sign of the infection has disappeared, she continues to be sick for a long time because her emotions are continuing the STH output.

Her attitude at the beginning of a cold is, "Oh, dear, dear me; here is one of these awful colds again; and now, woe is me, I'll be dreadfully sick all winter and into the summer. These colds are always so terrible and they get me down so hard. My back aches terribly; this headache is killing me; I know this will end up with kidney infection," and so forth.

It is not exaggerating a bit to say that Mrs. G—— frequently goes through all the agony of one of her long drawn-out colds without ever actually having a cold infection. I have seen her several times when she *thought* she was getting a cold. Actually there wasn't the least evidence of an infection present, but her emotional stimulation of STH was sufficient to produce a severe picture of being sick. The funny and truthful thing is that Mrs. G—— is just as sick as she says she is.

ACTH counteracts STH. A very opposite type of thing happens in a person who has an infection, but who has also the aggressively disagreeable type of emotions which stress ACTH. As we shall see in a moment, ACTH counteracts all the effects of STH, *including the defensive action against infection.* This person will have a severe infection which at first does not seem serious because ACTH is toning down the picture of being sick. This person will go on to develop all the complications in the book. We shall give a picture of such a person later.

➥ *Prolonged STH Stress — STH Stress Disease*

Prolonged, low-grade STH stress can be produced by a low-grade, chronic infection, such as one might have in the tonsils or in the infected root of a tooth; but prolonged STH stress is more apt to be produced by prolonged bad emotions. Whether it be a prolonged infection, or prolonged emotions, the final effect will be the same.

Under such low-grade STH stress, a person is tired, possibly has many aches and pains and other symptoms of the acute STH picture. With prolonged STH stress, new disease processes are started.

Dr. Selye became acquainted with these STH stress diseases by injecting STH into animals over a considerable period of time. Later he showed that these same changes could also be produced in animals by chronic infection, *or by prolonged emotions.* If he injected STH, and *conditioned* the animal with a high salt diet, the animal developed a malignant type of high blood pressure. If he *conditioned* the animal with a high protein diet, STH injection would then produce nephrosclerosis, a very severe type of kidney disease. If the conditioning factor were cold and wet to the joints, STH would produce rheumatoid arthritis, one of the worst varieties of arthritis. If conditioned by inhalations of mildly irritating bronchial inhalants (which by themselves had no bad aftereffects), the animals would develop asthma from the STH. If the conditioning were a spastic colon, STH would produce severe ulcerative colitis.

Other conditions, as well, are produced by STH, all of th them diseases of which we previously did not know the cause, such as periarteritis nodosa, lupus erythematosus disseminatus, and some others with high-sounding names. What is known as the "allergic state" is in some way (as yet undetermined) tied up with STH.

➤ *Asthma, An STH Stress Disease*

We begin to understand the role of emotions in asthma through the work of Dr. Selye. Time was, not too long ago, when we thought that all asthma was a sensitization to some protein outside the body. It was discouraging that in very few cases of asthma could such a connection be proven.

A few years ago we began to accept the obvious evidence that many cases of asthma definitely took their onset from a bronchial infection, and became worse with every renewed infection. And now we are seeing how, due to STH production, just as in the case of an infection, *asthma can be generated by the emotions, and be made worse by emotional tension.*

Mrs. D—— seemed to be a reasonably happy woman who was very active socially and civically in the medium-sized city in which she lived. Her children grew up. One of the daughters married badly and became a problem. Mrs. D——'s husband, at the foolish and experimental age of 53, had a perfectly foolish affair, which nearly prostrated Mrs. D——.

Finally, as an outlet or escape, Mrs. D—— went into office work, worked long hours at the job, and then worked into the wee hours at home, only to have her boss in the office tell her how perfectly awful her work was. After such a day, at her wits' end for recognition, feeling completely isolated and alone, and thoroughly tired, Mrs. D—— developed her first attack of asthma. The next day the asthma was bad enough to necessitate hospitalization. For the next six months Mrs. D—— was in the hospital, or hospitals (she went all over), without finding more than temporary relief.

On the surface she was a smiling, agreeable individual, seemingly with no great trouble, but fundamentally she was tense, discouraged, forlorn, and futile. The bottom had dropped out of her life. The office job was a last attempt to establish her usefulness and that failed. She tried hard to be jolly; it was a laudable effort. Her asthma then became her greatest apprehension. Her fears increased with each attack, and consequently, each attack became more severe and more difficult to control.

Infection stress versus emotional stress. It is easily possible to distinguish between the patients who have their asthma on an infectious basis and those who have it on an emotional basis. The latter are usually the more serious cases and the more difficult to control. It is very infrequent that a patient dies of infectious asthma, but I have seen a number die of emotionally-induced asthma.

It is also possible to separate patients whose rheumatoid arthritis is developed on an infection-stress basis from those whose malady is developed on an emotional-stress basis. Here again, the latter are the more severe.

➡ Sam and His Chronic STH Stress Disease

Sam, a farmer who has had a lifetime of dismal, discouraged, futile emotions — just the kind to stress STH — has had a long picture of STH stress disease. When Sam was comparatively young, he developed rheumatoid arthritis, not very severe, not crippling, but painful. Later he developed asthma, again not so severely that he couldn't go on working. Later he developed high blood pressure, and now he has nephrosclerosis. One can say, and with truth, that all these illnesses must have helped to produce Sam's morose outlook. But the most important truth is that Sam's outlook was responsible for the illness.

➤ *The Adrenocorticotrophic Hormone*

ACTH. The ACTH (*adrenocorticotrophic hormone*) of the pituitary does not act directly on the body, but on the adrenal glands, stimulating the latter to produce cortisone which acts on the body in many remarkable ways. However, since cortisone is produced under the stimulation of ACTH, we will refer to its action as being that of ACTH.

The chief effect of ACTH is to oppose the action of STH. By giving ACTH in large enough amounts, one can completely counteract the effect of STH — the inflammatory effect, the defense against infection, the picture of "being sick." This action is one of the most dramatic things that has ever been demonstrated in medicine. One has to see it to believe it.

For instance, a patient may be sick with a *severe* lobar pneumonia. His temperature is 105°F., his face is flushed, his lips are blue, his respiration is rapid, he has a stabbing pain in the chest, he is tired and exhausted and aches all over; the skin is dry, the tongue furred, the eyes glassy.

If the doctor gives him sufficient ACTH intravenously, within a matter of a few hours, the temperature is normal, the flush is gone, the pain is gone, the tiredness is gone, he breathes easily, he feels strong, he can walk around with ease, and eat a good meal. He looks as though he had never been sick. One would say, looking at him, that he is cured.

But all that has actually happened is that the STH effects

have been cancelled out — *the infection is still there,* now unopposed by the defensive action of STH. If one kept giving ACTH, the infection would go on like a prairie fire. *Even though the individual felt well,* lung abscesses would develop, or empyema, and the patient would certainly have a fatal termination.

ACTH would have the same symptom-relieving effect in any infection and would produce a fatal outcome. That is why one is careful not to give ACTH to a person who has ever had tuberculosis for fear of lighting up the old infection.

However, it is quite a different thing if one gives ACTH to a person who has STH stress disease. In that case, there is no infection. For example, if one gives ACTH to a person who has rheumatoid arthritis or bronchial asthma, the asthma or the arthritis will completely disappear — as long as the administration of ACTH is continued. But the asthma and arthritis reappear again when the ACTH is stopped, because nothing has been done to stop the STH stress.

ACTH has been used, and successfully, in all the STH stress diseases. However, there is one very great limitation to its use in the present state of our knowledge — that is, that the continued use of ACTH leads to ACTH stress disease just as STH did.

ACTH stress disease. The only two ways that we know a person can get ACTH stress disease is either by prolonged injection of ACTH in one of the STH stress diseases or through prolonged emotional stress. The type of emotions that stimulate ACTH are the aggressively unpleasant emotions, the emotions one gets by driving oneself relentlessly toward a goal, or the emotion of militant dissatisfaction.

A common ACTH stress effect is peptic ulcer. Practically every animal receiving ACTH for any length of time develops an ulcer, and the same is true in humans. Ulcer is an executive's disease because the emotions that stress ACTH are the emotions an executive is apt to have. However, executives are not the only ones who have the particular brand of emotions necessary to get an ulcer.

Anyone who is aggressively dissatisfied is a candidate. In some very noisy occupations, such as a body-grinding department in an automobile body plant, a high percentage of workers develop an ulcer. Ulcers can easily be produced in rats by subjecting them to irritating high-pitched noises.

But let's look at a surprising chemical effect of ACTH overproduction, remembering that there is no chemical activity in the body (which is a tremendously complicated chemical plant) that is not in some way under the direction of the endocrine system, and realizing that the effect of emotional endocrine stress on chemical actions is both terrific and manifold.

An important ACTH stress experiment. Dr. Selye and his co-workers selected two groups of Montreal children. One group was chosen from homes in which there was a terrific amount of trouble and in which everyone was unhappy, including the children. The other group of children were chosen from homes that were happy and in which the children were happy.

These two groups were fed in the university mess hall on the same diet, a very excellent, well-prepared diet. Dieticians were present to see that the children ate their meals and liked their food. Excepting for their meals in the mess hall, all the children went their usual ways and lived as they were accustomed to live.

At the end of a given time, it was found that the children from the happy homes had gained weight well above the normal average for the age, whereas the group of children from the unhappy homes, although they were on the same diet, had not kept their weight gain up to normal for their age. During the period of the experiment, it was determined by actual assay that the unhappy children were stressing their pituitaries to produce an excessive amount of ACTH, this in turn produced cortisone, and cortisone affected the metabolism of protein in an interesting way. The amino acids, which is the form in which protein is absorbed from the intestine into the blood, were changed in increasing amounts into glucose by the ACTH, and less than the usual amount into protein for body building. Many of the unhappy children were at times in a negative nitrogen balance, that is, they were losing more protein from their bodies than they were making, in spite of their excellent diet.

The reverse was true of the children from the happy homes. They were stimulating their pituitaries optimally. Their amino acids were being changed into protein in optimal amounts. The stressed children also had a greater number of infections during the time of the observation because ACTH over-production was also lowering the resistance to infection, which is, you remember, dependent on STH.

➤ The Picture of Chronic ACTH Stress Disease

One sees people who are chronically dissatisfied all their lives. They are aggressively resentful — quick to be upset — quick to be hurt — long to hold a grudge — always struggling to change something or somebody the way *they* want.

Mrs. V—— was exactly such a person. Her life was a chain of illnesses, each a new ACTH stress disease. In her girlhood she had a succession of boils, colds, and abscesses. No one could understand why she had no resistance to infection. She didn't like her teachers, or the way they ran the school. She often became angry at her schoolmates. She became a store clerk, but contracted tuberculosis.

After a period in the sanatorium, she married. Her husband then became the central object of her dissatisfaction, principally because his earning power cramped her possibilities. When I first saw her, she had an ulcer and a tremendously irritable colon. The ulcer refused to heal over a period of years, even under the most meticulous medical care. She was in such a continual emotional dither that even the usually willing surgeons refused to perform an ulcer operation. But over the years the cicatrix produced by the ulcer gradually closed the outlet of the stomach, and surgery finally became an emergency.

She did poorly after surgery, healed slowly, and never really pulled herself back together. Immediately after surgery she had an infection of the lung, which gradually became worse until she had multiple lung abscesses. A portion of the lung finally had to be removed. Next she had rectal fistulas. At the age of 50, she had a painful and well-developed osteoporosis. One cannot predict what this poor woman will develop next. Her illness, of course, has roughened her disposition, but the important relationship is the other way around.

The thing which immediately strikes us about people like Mrs. V—— is their personality, in which emotional stress stands out like the nose on their face. Not infrequently these people take to alcohol to give themselves temporary relief from the effects of their emotions. They readily become chronic alcoholics, and develop cirrhosis of the liver because, with alcohol as a conditioning factor, cirrhosis occurs as the result of ACTH over-production.

➤ *The Future of Endocrine Research*

In this chapter, we have considered emotional stress as it affects only two of the hormones of the pituitary gland, and the effects of these two hormones only in a very sketchy way. What happens when combinations of hormones are relatively stressed in differing amounts is still a subject for future investigation. In fact, the subject of endocrine stress has been barely opened. But already a new era is imminent in the treatment of stress disease.

THE HIGHSPOTS OF CHAPTER IV

The endocrine glands (pituitary, adrenals, thyroid, parathyroids, thymus, pancreas, and gonads) govern and regulate the normal functions of our bodies. But they also start and regulate the body's reaction to stressing, threatening forces.

The pituitary is the master endocrine that controls all the others.

The pituitary responds to stress by producing one or more of its twelve hormones in increased amounts. Common stresses are bacterial or viral infection, exposure to heat, cold, moisture, dryness, or high altitudes, muscular overexertion, starvation, and many others. But the most important stress of all is that of the stressing emotions. Emotional stress can be greater than any other stress. Emotions usually act for a longer time than do other stressors, and they can produce the same effects as *any* other type of stress.

An infection stresses the pituitary to overproduce **STH**. The emotions of defeat, futility, and discouragement have exactly the same action. The immediate effects of **STH** are tiredness, general aching, nausea, weakness, as well as inflammations and defense against bacteria. Small increases of **STH** over a long period of time produce a variety of conditions: asthma, rheumatoid arthritis, high blood pressure, nephrosclerosis, periarteritis, lupus erythematosis, and others.

The aggressively unpleasant type of emotions, such as an executive must often have to be an executive, or that a crusader or reformer might have, stress the pituitary's production of **ACTH**. **ACTH** stops all the effects of **STH**, including the defense against infection. **ACTH** also produces peptic ulcers, a variety of diabetes, a diminution of the available protein in the body, and other changes.

In short, consider what you're doing to yourself before you give vent to an emotion.

5. GOOD EMOTIONS ARE YOUR BEST MEDICINE

➤ *Good Emotions Are the Best Medicine*

In the few years since medical men began to understand the mechanism of functional disease, they have been so occupied with telling the bad effects of the wrong emotions that they have neglected to stress the effects of the good emotions. These last are just as beneficial to the person having them as the wrong emotions are detrimental.

As a matter of fact, the good emotions are *the greatest power for your good health* that we know anything about. The only medicines we have whose power is comparable to the power of good emotions are the antibiotics (such as penicillin), on the one hand, and ACTH and cortisone, on the other. The usefulness of ACTH and cortisone are limited by their possible bad effects. We have not learned to give ACTH or cortisone without producing the ill effects of ACTH stress disease.

The body knows the secret of optimal hormone balance. We do not. *But there is one way you have of achieving op-*

*timal hormone balance. That is to provide your body with
the stimulus of the pleasant and cheerful group of emotions.*

The physiologic effects of the good emotions are just as
great in the right direction as the effects of the bad emotions
are in the wrong direction. The "medicinal" value of the
good emotions cannot be overestimated.

Dr. Paul White of Boston, one of the country's leading
heart specialists, was one of the first men to call attention to
this fact.

➡ *The Powerful Effect of Good Emotions*

Dr. White, in *The Annals of Internal Medicine* for De-
cember, 1951, gave examples to illustrate his point. In the
days before we knew anything about ACTH, he had a patient,
a young mother with two children and a drunken, worthless
husband, who developed a serious case of rheumatic fever.
She had been in bed three years, and her doctors gave her,
at most, another year to live.

Rheumatic fever is another disease which Dr. Hans Selye
has produced in animals with STH and the proper conditioning; and today this young woman would receive ACTH or
cortisone, with resultant amelioration of her illness. But at
the time of this story it was, of course, not available.

The young woman's emotional state was at a terrifically
low ebb. Even her will to get well had left. Then a blessing
in disguise occurred; her husband pulled out for parts unknown, leaving the mother and two children without even
the meagre support he had been giving. The patient rose to
the occasion, and the occasion pulled her out of the doldrums.

When Dr. White came to see her, she said firmly, "Dr.
White, I'm going to get out of bed and support my two children."

Dr. White answered, "My dear lady, I wish you could, but
your heart wouldn't stand it."

Now, it wasn't, mind you, that Dr. White was underestimating her heart. A man like Dr. Paul White knows a heart when he examines one, and knows what can be expected of it. But Dr. White was underestimating the physiologic effects of ACTH (which were unknown at the time) and the possibility that certain emotions could stimulate the production of ACTH and produce a normal hormonal spectrum. Despite Dr. White's advice, the young woman, with courage, determination, enthusiasm, and cheerfulness, got out of bed and went to work. She supported and reared her two children for eight years.

Any observant physician can tell you similar stories out of his own practice. One commonly sees such examples after surgery. One of the surgeons in our clinic did a very extensive and difficult piece of surgery to save a man's life from a malignancy. Three days after surgery the surgeon asked me to see the patient, saying, "The man is going to die."

I looked at his hospital chart, and from the record it certainly did look as though he were going to die. I went into his room. The man was conscious, but that was about all.

I said, "Henry, how are you today?"

Henry pulled a generous smile, put a glow of determined enthusiasm into his eyes (I don't know where he got the strength to do it) and answered with a genuine sincere feeling: "Fine! I'm going to be out of here in a few days."

And that remained Henry's attitude. He got well. If he had accepted the emotions of despair and defeat that his condition warranted, I am sure Henry would have died.

Another remarkable individual I will never forget was a middle-aged lady who was in the hospital because of an uncontrollable hemorrhagic disease. Every day her condition grew seemingly worse. Every time I came on the wards I no longer expected to find her alive. But whenever I asked her how she felt — "I feel fine and I want to sit up today. I'm going home soon." She maintained that cheerfulness and courage. She got well; not because of any treatment I gave her, but because of the treatment her emotions gave her.

➡ *The Good Emotions Produce an Optimal Hormone Balance*

These people stimulate their pituitaries in just the proper optimal way to produce a balance of hormones such as we cannot achieve by giving the hormones artificially. Don't forget, these are the same hormones, just as powerful and just as effective, as those we were talking about in the last chapter. But the right kind of emotions produce these hormones in the right amounts, just as the wrong kind of emotions produce them in harmful amounts.

➡ *Good Emotions Work Miracles*

Our knowledge of hormones, incomplete and fragmentary though it still is, sheds light on many seemingly miraculous cures. As we understand it better, our natural world becomes increasingly wonderful, and thousands and thousands of times more amazing than the ancients thought it to be.

Let's take a case for illustration. Before the days of anti-microbials, a colored man had a kidney infection. Of course, the antimicrobials would now clear this up in 24 hours. But in 1934 it was a serious affair. The man had always been irritable and aggressively disagreeable. He gradually grew worse. He had the type of emotions which stimulate ACTH; he was counteracting any defensive action STH might have. He was providing no resistance to the infection.

Then a voodoo healer got hold of the man. He changed the man's emotions to the cheerful ones, gave him enthusiasm, hope, and a terrific courage (all of which, mind you, I had been unable to do). What happened in the man was that an optimal balance of hormones allowed the maximum defensive mobilization of STH. The body's own immunity reactions were all the treatment we had at that time. The man got better.

The same effect would have occurred had his emotions

been changed to the good by any other means — for example, a romantic love affair. The important thing was not the means, but the right kind of emotions.

This kind of thing has been going on ever since the human race started. We are only beginning to appreciate its true significance.

➤ *The Good Emotions Work in Two Ways*

Don't forget that the good emotions have two general effects. First, they replace the bad emotions which were producing stress effects; and secondly, they produce their own pituitary effect which is an optimal balance of endocrine function. It is this optimal balance which produces the state which we human beings have always called, "Gee, I feel good!" But the first effect, that of replacing the bad emotions and their stress effects, is equally important.

➤ *Why Not Live?*

Once we appreciate that healthful living is more a matter of having the right kind of emotions than anything else, it becomes apparent that the most important aspect of living consists in training and handling our emotions.

So far, education has consisted largely in educating our intelligence, which is quite necessary also. But one can have a very high intelligence, and very bad emotions, and live perfectly miserably. If it were a matter of one *or* the other, life would be sweeter with good emotions and low intelligence.

As a matter of fact, if one goes about it right, it is *easier* to acquire good emotions than a good intelligence. And there is actually no need for anyone to have bad emotions. So many people do have bad emotions because, for so many thousands of years, we have neglected to train people in emotional control.

THIS CHAPTER IN A NUTSHELL

The healthy emotions have just as great an effect on the pituitary as the stressing emotions do. Their effect is just as powerful in the direction of good health as the effect of the stressing emotions is toward bad health.

The healthy emotions, such as equanimity, resignation, courage, determination, and cheerfulness, stimulate the pituitary to produce an optimal hormone spectrum, and effect with far greater power for good health than any drug, or set of drugs, that we know anything about.

6. YOUR FUNDAMENTAL AND YOUR SUPERFICIAL EMOTIONS

➡ *You Have Two Emotional Levels at All Times*

There is one more important point to understand about emotions if we are to understand their effect on us.

We all are always having emotions on two different levels at the same moment. Or you might say that we have two layers of emotions, an outside layer that everyone sees, and an inside deep layer that no one sees unless he has learned to spy beneath the surface. The emotions in the deep underlying layer we may call the FUNDAMENTAL emotions.[1] Those in the outside layer we may call the SUPERFICIAL emotions. We can best understand these two varieties by an example.

Let us suppose that this morning you committed a misdeed or a crime. Let us also suppose it is your first crime, and you are obviously not a hardened criminal. You are afraid. You have a feeling of guilt. You wish mightily that the moment of your dreadful deed might be blotted away, or relived without crime. Most of all, of course, you are expecting to be appre-

---

[1] These are what the psychiatrist terms the *affect*.

hended by the police, who are on your trail. For the next hours, for the next days, perhaps, you will constantly have a FUNDAMENTAL emotion of fear-anxiety-remorse.

The emotion *is* the manifestation; without the bodily changes, there would be no emotion. And so, every minute of those waitful, apprehensive, hours or days, the emotion will be tightening muscles, overstimulating the endocrine glands. Because of these manifestations you will, doubtless, feel unwell.

There may be moments during those hours when your mind will necessarily have to be on other subjects, and there may be a play of SUPERFICIAL emotions, some of which may be seemingly cheerful and pleasant, even though the FUNDAMENTAL emotion is continuing its manifestations unchecked. There are moments when to an outsider you *seem* happy, your joking sincere, and your heart light. But inside, all the time, you know the real state of affairs, because you can feel that dreadful sensation in your stomach even when you are laughing at someone's joke.

The FUNDAMENTAL emotion continues through your day like a backdrop on a stage; the SUPERFICIAL emotions flit about before the backdrop, and hold the stage for their little time; but before them, and during them, and after them, the backdrop of FUNDAMENTAL emotions continues.

➤ Fundamental Emotions Have the Greatest Effect

Such FUNDAMENTAL emotions have more to do with bringing on functional disease than do the superficial emotions, because they are constant, because they are often very basically unhappy, and because they often continue for a very long time, longer than the event or situation that started them.

FUNDAMENTAL emotions may last an entire lifetime, constantly producing symptoms of disease, without the person being precisely aware that the FUNDAMENTAL emotion exists, and without those near and with him sensing its presence

For example, Walter, age 27, was a friendly young man, likable and pleasant, and generally regarded by the people who patronized his gas station as a happy fellow. To those who knew him better, like his wife, he had moments when he looked apprehensive, became pensive with a serious look in his eyes as though he were looking for something to happen. Not even his friends knew he had a chronic diarrhea which had grown steadily worse ever since he was six years old.

At age five, Walter was riding with his father on a wagon. Suddenly, (there was a storm coming), a bolt of lightning killed his father and the two horses. From then on, Walter was never without a FUNDAMENTAL emotion of fear and anxiety, which manifested itself in part in the colon. The FUNDAMENTAL emotion was present regardless of what his SUPERFICIAL emotions might be.

➡ Battle Emotions

Battles or other dreadful frightening events, may produce emotions which carry on for years, even though the person's surface may often appear smooth, cheerful, and unruffled.

➡ Fundamental Emotions from Unfilled Basic Needs

One of the commonest causes of a prolonged, severely unhappy FUNDAMENTAL emotion is an unfilled basic psychological need, six of which — love, security, recognition, creative expression, new experiences, self-esteem — we discuss in Chapter 14.

➡ Fundamental Emotions from Immaturity

Another common cause of unfavorable FUNDAMENTAL emotions is immaturity and the consequent problems which an immature personality manufactures for itself. Some of these we discuss in Chapter 7.

➤ *Cheerful Fundamental Emotions*

Fortunate is the person who has a layer of FUNDAMENTAL emotions that are habitually cheerful. He has what we call a cheerful disposition, and it is worth more to him than wealth of all the world. In fact, it is hardly ever found where there is wealth.

A cheerful and pleasant disposition, that is to say, happy FUNDAMENTAL emotions, should be the central aim in the raising of children. Give them this, and they will have more than they can ever get in any other way. If you've grown up without a naturally happy disposition, it is not too late to cultivate one. It calls for the constant practice of a few principles that are simple, and which we will present in Part II of this book.

POINTS TO REMEMBER IN THIS CHAPTER

Each of us has, at all times, two different sets of emotions. Each set is making its own physical and chemical changes in our bodies.

The SUPERFICIAL emotions are the set we have out on the surface from minute to minute, such as our radiant pleasantness when someone gives us a box of candy.

The FUNDAMENTAL, or deeper emotions, are the ones that are the background of the world we are living in — the feeling that persists inside us when our son is a prisoner in the enemy's hands, or a feeling of the dark dismal view of the world our parents may have given us, or the general tone of apprehension we have when a loved one is sick.

A person may have an outwardly genial manner and yet have a set of fundamental emotions which are doing him no good. Sometimes the fundamental emotions may be the result of unfulfilled psychological needs, sometimes they may result from the effects of immaturity, and sometimes they may be due to factors which the person does not admit to exist.

The only satisfactory fundamental emotions are those that go with the person who has acquired a truly happy disposition, who has learned to maintain emotions of equanimity, resignation, courage, determination, and cheerfulness.

PART II.   *HOW TO CURE YOUR*
                    EMOTIONALLY
                    INDUCED ILLNESS

7.

YOU CAN ACHIEVE
EMOTIONAL STASIS

➡ *There Has Always Been E. I. I.*

There is probably no more emotionally induced illness to-day, nor any greater amount of emotional stress, than there was in days gone by. The world has always been full of it. People in bygone days didn't meet the ups-and-downs of living with any less emotional stress than people do today. And although we of the mid-20th Century have such stresses today as the world political situation, practically every age had its world situations and its wars, in some ages much more constantly than we have had. Although we have the stress of an excessive amount of publicity on diseases of all varieties, past ages had the greater stress of smallpox, tuberculosis, diphtheria, plague, typhoid, dysentery, osteomyelitis, and many other miserable conditions which today are rare indeed.

No age ever "had it as good" as ours; no age has ever been as free from want, or as free from the effects of just plain weather, as we are. Every age has had emotional stress.

We, in the United States, probably have less emotional stress today than any people ever before in the history of the world. That isn't the way you usually hear it. We pay more attention to the stress people are under today because we are beginning to learn about its importance. We are going to be able to reduce people's emotional stress in the future just as we have reduced contagious disease. We are just beginning to learn how.

➡ Emotional Stasis Versus Trouble

The most surprising thing about people who have E. I. I. is that usually they do not have a great amount of trouble. You'd think they would, wouldn't you? You would think the rule might be expressed in equations something like these:

- Much trouble in life = emotionally induced illness.
- Little trouble = No E. I. I.

But this is not true. A large amount of trouble may, of course, help bring on E. I. I. but *the majority* of patients with E. I. I. actually have very little real trouble.

The chief factor that brings on E. I. I. is that the patient has never learned to maintain good healthy emotions in just plain, ordinary, everyday living — in those situations where there are only the usual daily varieties of trouble every one of us has all the time. That factor is responsible for the disease in 90 per cent of E. I. I. patients.

They have never learned to produce a good, healthy stream of emotions in the face of the changing situations they meet in ordinary living. By ordinary living I mean having to make a living, having to meet problems of income and expenditure, having to discipline a family, having to iron out an occasional altercation. Death in the family must be faced, too, since that is a part of all ordinary living.

These patients have never learned the art of *emotional stasis;* they meet living with emotional stress. *Emotional stasis* is the ability to meet a wide variety of life situations, the bad with the good, with emotions like equanimity, resignation, courage, determination, cheerfulness, and pleasantness. The person who lacks emotional stasis meets most of his situations, good with bad, with emotions like anxiety, fear, apprehension, discouragement, disappointment, and frustration.

But, of course, what we are saying about the E. I. I. patient who doesn't have a good healthy stream of emotions applies to almost all of us, since practically everyone, at some time or other (including you and me, dear reader), has E. I. I.

➧ *Emotional Stress Is Due to an Educational Failure*

So many of us today, as well as most everyone in the past, has lacked emotional stasis because man leaves to chance a quality that must be learned. The only way a person can develop emotional stasis is through the right kind of education. But the right kind of education *does not exist*.

There is no place you can go to learn emotional stasis. There should be, but there isn't. And there isn't because it has taken mankind until the middle of the 20th Century to learn what emotional stasis is. Education in emotional stasis is coming, and some day our descendants will learn it in school. But that doesn't help you and me right now, does it?

The family influence. A person's total education, of course, includes much, much more than what he learns in the schools he attends. Our *most important* educational influence is the family we are brought up in. And there are many, many families whose effect on their children is a terrible and ruinous one. Most families develop strong emotional stress. There are many exceptions, certainly, but by and large, our families are educational flops of the first water.

Influence of our friends. The second most important educational factor each of us has are the people who live within our circle, those with whom we play, talk, visit, work, fight, love. This circle includes authors who enter our private worlds through their books, even though they may be dead. If we are lucky, some strong enlightened individual enters our circle and influences us in the development of a healthy attitude or two. But most of the people who stream through our lives are mediocre and full of educational stress.

Influence of our schools. Our schools are our third most important educational influence. The schools do not even pretend to do anything about emotional stasis. I think they will before long. There are several forward-looking educators who are beginning to plan for it and think about it. The central goal in our education should be to fit people for living full, enjoyable lives, instead of having them run a marathon of seventy years of emotional stress.*

Influence of the church. The churches are our fourth most important educational influence. Like the schools they, too, do not have a conscious program for developing emotional stasis. Religion, as it is conceived by the churches, does not provide its members, or its clergy, with the type of emotions which save them from E. I. I. The clergy, in my experience, have functional disease as much as any other group. Only among the Quakers and the Christian Scientists is there an appreciable lack of E. I. I. I say this without prejudice; I belong to neither denomination.

➡ *"Maturity" Is Another Name for Emotional Stasis*

The same educational influences which make for emotional stasis also make for the thing we call "maturity." An education that would provide a person with emotional stasis would also provide him with maturity. Emotional stasis is the emotional counterpart of being mature.

It has been only recently that psychologists have come to understand, and to be able to state, just what maturity consists of. *Maturity* is just what it sounds like — the ability to react to life situations in ways that are more beneficial than the ways in which a child would react. *Emotional stasis* is exactly the same thing. *Emotional stress* is what a child produces when faced with a menacing situation; a mature person has *emotional stasis* in the same situations.

---

* A recent book, *Building Your Life,* by Judson T. and Mary G. Landis, published by Prentice-Hall, Inc., New York, is a valuable aid for adolescents in the development of a mature life. It is an important book for all who are interested in this subject.

Psychologists have also become aware that few or no people are fully mature — there is some place in their personality where they still react like children, with childish stress emotions. There are only a very few people that even approximate full maturity simply because there is no organized educational effort to make us mature. It is left to chance. A few people are fortunate enough to fall into the hands of very sensible individuals who can show them how to achieve some degree of maturity, but even so, it is never the complete course.

A man in the forefront of his profession or industry will display to the public a fairly well-rounded maturity in the sense we are going to describe. But somewhere in his makeup, there is apt to be a very immature spot; in regard to some things that he meets in his living he will have reactions characteristic and worthy of a child.

Some public office holders, men in the headlines every day, are extremely immature in very fundamental ways. Once the public learns what maturity and immaturity are, men like these will no longer reach high office. They will be spotted for what they are — immature fakes — and society will be spared the nonsense and nuisance they produce.

Once our society makes it a point to train people to reach maturity and emotional stasis, there will be many, many more people reaching fairly well-rounded maturity. The entire complexion of public as well as private life will be changed for our great good.

➡ A Common Misconception of Maturity

I would like first of all to invite your attention to a common variety of immaturity which a certain group of men regard as maturity. This particular variety of immaturity causes a great deal of trouble to society, to the man who has it, and to the woman unlucky enough to have married the big stiff.

The most typical example of this immature hero is the rough don't-give-a-damn-for-anything he-man-bravado individual who plays a kind of a four-year-old cowboy-badman game all his life. These are the gangsters, the bad men whom radio and television play up to their youthful audiences, and to whose activities the newspapers devote reams of copy.

This typical bad-man immaturity occurs much more frequently, in watered-down form, in the he-man who keeps his family at home while he participates in fishing, hunting, small gambling — the man forever going out with the fellows for this and that, and a drink.

I mention this group particularly because it is surprising how frequently their immaturity figures in the emotional stress of their wives and children. There are many variations of the immaturity represented by these two types. Every town has many of them around.

The tougher they are, and the tougher they act, the more immature and childish they actually are. Their babyhood crops out terrifically whenever one of them has to be stuck with a needle, or has to submit to some form of minor surgery without an anesthesia. They just can't take it. I've seen some of the "toughest guys" in St. Louis, men who were in the headlines of gangsterism, carry on like babies when they were faced with an intravenous needle.

Their toughness is, of course, a front they kid themselves with. They simply can't take it. They can't stand stress of any kind, and they turn easily to drink, which is an ineffective way of easing tension. And so their concept of maturity comes to contain the idea of hard, regular drinking, just as it contained the idea of smoking when they were ten or eleven. Their concept of maturity, furthermore, contains the idea of "handling their women rough," or with indifference. It's a pity the law lets them marry.

These fellows come into the clinic when their concepts of maturity are beginning to show the strain — that is, in their forties or fifties. At that age, most of them are pretty poor physical specimens; they are children in every department of living. They have been children so long and so thoroughly they cannot conceive of any other state.

Their poor wives come to the clinic a little earlier — in their thirties and early forties. Their children come to the clinic still earlier. There are no problem children, only problem parents.

➤ The Qualities That Make for Maturity *

1. **Responsible independence, the first criterion of maturity.** A necessary step in growing up is the development of the ability to assume responsibility independently of father, mother, and other protective agencies. Long years of childhood, especially in families where protective concern is carried to an extreme, develop the tendency to keep depending on someone else. Many parents, especially mothers, strongly foster dependence when they should be molding independence.

Those who grow up with a dependent attitude sooner or later have a hard time. A wife runs to mother with every squall, and with every responsibility of marriage. This running to mother, and her consequent intervention, irritates the husband more and more. The marriage gradually falls apart at the seams, and everybody in the play, wife, husband, and mother-in-law, have emotionally induced illness.

Then there is the well-known boy who is made to depend on his mother. As he grows into his teens the boys make fun of him, and he feels that his dependency on his mother is a weakness. To prove his strength to himself and to his fellows he becomes a super kind of a regular guy, which is only a step away from gangsterism. After that there is petty crime, and trouble all over the landscape, with emotionally induced illness in mother, father, son.

Other people start out leaning heavily on parents, friends, relatives. When these supports are removed, they look for support in alcohol. They always have E. I. I.

---

* For the qualities of maturity discussed in this chapter I am indebted to Dr. Leon J. Saul, *Emotional Maturity*. Philadelphia: J. B. Lippincott Company, 1947.

2. **Maturity means a giving, rather than a receiving, attitude.** A characteristically childhood attitude is to want to receive, to be given desired things. In this immaturity, the person does things with the attitude, "What is this going to get me?" This is a springboard into mean, crabby emotions. As they get older they no longer receive as they did when they were children, although they still think in terms of what they can get. They are in a dead-end alley that leads to intense desire, and finally to intense frustration.

Two unmarried sisters had always lived together, supported by a fair competence left them by their father. Then an old uncle, who had always been a troublemaker, died, and left his farm to the older (by two years), with the provision that it would pass to the younger when the older died. But the younger sister wanted to get her share at once, and demanded that the farm be sold and divided equally. But the older sister had the farm, and she wanted to keep it. Over this, they quarreled. They left each other to live alone.

Today, they are both miserable with emotionally induced illness, and will continue to be until they both mature enough to want to give rather than to get. So far, after ten years, neither has matured. They are both slightly under fifty and have many years of ill health to look forward to. Furthermore, both have lawyers, and the litigation they are in may well cost them the farm the troublemaking uncle hung around their necks.

Maturity brings with it a rich concern: how to make the living of others more enjoyable. With this concern, horizons, vision, and sympathy broaden. The person with such maturity is not living in a little closet, grasping and pulling everything possible into its dark confines. He is roaming the sunshine and the great wide world, finding other people interesting and worth the effort of knowing and giving.

Actually, in his mean position, the constant receiver never learns what great enjoyment giving can bring; he does learn how his cramped, grasping, tight emotions produce almost constant ill health.

3. Maturity means leaving egotism and competitiveness behind. The childish attitude is, "I've got something you haven't got," or "I can do something you can't do," or "My father can lick your father." There are many people who never lose this childish constellation of egoism and competitiveness. They are always hard to get along with because they are always pitting themselves against everybody else. They never develop a kindly cooperativeness. They are obnoxious as partners in a business, they are irritative in a gathering, they are quarrelsome in a twosome.

The over-competitive person. The person who constantly compares himself (in jealous competition) with everyone else is destined to be a miserable human being. He constantly generates envy, hurt pride, and hostility in himself and in others.

The irascible, headline-seeking politicians who are constantly imposing their will on everyone else are of this breed. If you watch their movements in Washington, they are frequently over in Bethesda Medical Center (which Congress built for the Navy and Congressmen) being "checked-over" or being treated for "sinus trouble" or having an operation for a substitution diagnosis of E. I. I.

These men consider themselves leaders, and highly mature. If their voting public only knew it, they are highly immature — immature in the category we are speaking of, as well as in most of the other categories of maturity. The continual blustering of this class of politicians produces anxiety in themselves, as well as in those they bluster against. In their innate childishness, they are striving to be something that isn't in them — mature men.

Competition can be valuable. Competition, to a degree, has its place in living. But when it becomes too strong and all-pervasive, it defeats its own purpose. It produces anxiety, strain, stress, and remorse, and effectively precludes enjoyment even in those who are successful.

One of the elements in modern business and industry that produces a great amount of E. I. I. is the competition between those striving to get to the top. The managers of local stores in large chain systems are frequently seeking medical attention because they are pitted against each other on the sales sheet in their effort to rise above the local store. The same is true in banks and industries. Those who manage to go up in their system suffer from the strained aggression, and often have ulcers. Those who fail suffer frustration and its resulting fatigue and prolonged headache. Who wins? I don't know; I haven't as yet seen any of them win.

The system is at fault. We can say without exaggeration that a system of this kind is childish and immature. We may hope that with the passage of time it will perhaps grow up and develop a kindlier and more cooperative feeling for human beings. Today it is the ruin of many of the lives of those who serve under it. Is big business, big industry, pursued solely for its own sake, worth the human price? I am inclined to think it is not.

The building of a mature human being, that is to say, a happy human being, is the only honest and worthy business and industry that any of us have a right to have. Any form of industry and business that provides its human beings with an unhealthy set of emotions is as immature and socially undesirable as the childishly egotistical and competitive individual.

Dick was the manager of a local chain store. The store he was running was in competition with the other stores in other towns. To get to be district manager, Dick had to outsell the other managers of the competing stores. For a rather poor salary, he worked night and day. He developed an ulcer, but he became district manager. There were some other fellows in other stores who developed the same kind of ulcers without becoming district manager. In every competition, someone has to lose. Then they develop something beside an ulcer. But Dick became district manager. His pay was then a little bigger, but he had much bigger worries, and much bigger competition. He worked and stewed harder than ever, but his district fell behind someone else's district, and he didn't make the next promotion he was hoping for. So came the frustration of defeat with fatigue, constipation, headache, insomnia.

Then there are people like Mrs. B—— who has an ego as big and rough as the Tetons. Every contact she makes with anyone else is a competition in which she demonstrates that she is just a little smarter. She has outrun and outpunted her husband so long that the poor fellow drags around with a pitiful inferiority complex. At any meeting in which the chairman is silly enough to open the discussion, she rises militantly to her feet and starts out to change something, or someone. She is a frightful power in the woman's club, a caution in the P.T.A., and a terrific headache in her bridge club. The city hall shudders every time she passes through. But nature is a balance of compensations. She pays dearly for her immaturity. Every so often at night, she privately develops a most disabling spell, which lasts until morning, and which leaves her deflated for a couple of days. The trouble with Mrs. B—— is that she hasn't matured enough to become kindly cooperative with other human beings. She is a child in that respect. "My mamma can lick your mamma" is about where this aspect of her education stopped. Watch them sometime — the people who chronically run things are themselves run by the chronic effects of their own emotions.

4. **Maturity in sex.** The childhood sexual attitude is one of genital satisfaction in the interests of self-love without the realization that sex is part of the larger experience of mating. This, like every other experience involving two human beings, becomes mature only when kindliness, sympathy, and mutual cooperativeness enter into it.

Sexual immaturity is so very common largely because of the fears and inhibitions that block rational efforts at sex education. The schools, the families, the churches give the individual no organized instruction for handling sex in the course of his living. Most of the instruction is left to disreputable sources, and is of a disreputable flavor. Little wonder that so few grow up into sexual maturity.

Two types of sexual immaturity. One type of sexual immaturity is a hysterical fear of sex and all it connotes.

Rose was an extremely pretty girl who lived in a very rough neighborhood. Endeavoring to help Rose survive the tough neighborhood, her mother put a tremendous fear of sex into the girl. When Rose was married, years later, she was incapable of mating. Her husband tried every possible approach with infinite patience. But Rose withdrew more and more, physically and mentally. Knowing she was not a successful wife made her feel very guilty and inadequate. She developed a nonspecific ulcerative colitis and at one time she was hospitalized for an entire year.

Quite the opposite variety of sexual immaturity consists of making sexuality the most important thing in living.

Darlene grew up in a family that, in a vulgar sort of way, made a fetish of being uninhibited. The only kind of humor Darlene ever heard was the very broad, sexy variety. There was no restriction put on sexy movies; there were always mother's sexy magazines around the house. The visitors who came to the house were of the sophisticated variety whose sophistication runs to sex.

Before Darlene was old enough to date, her mother thought it cute for her to go to dances and shows with boys. Darlene became pregnant before her time, and dragged the family through one affair after another. So far, and she is still only 35, Darlene has made herself enough trouble for a lifetime, and she is capable of filling up three more. She is complaining of one thing and another all the time, and has practically leased a chair in a doctor's waiting room.

5. Maturity means living higher than the level of hostile aggressiveness. There are some who regard hostile aggressiveness — anger, hate, cruelty, and belligerency — as strength. Quite the opposite is true. These are childish arrests, gross forms of immaturity, signs of weakness, evidences of fear and frustration.

Childishly aggressive men. Children, living in a world in which they are relatively impotent, feel weak, dependent, and insecure. When they are frustrated in their desires by discipline, they react with anger, hate, belligerency, and, if they can, with cruelty. Many people grow into adulthood without growing out of this form of hostile aggressiveness. They remain cruel and belligerent because they still feel weak, dependent, and insecure. They *are* weak; they haven't learned how to be strong. Only the strong can be gentle. The men who usurp power in the governments of the world, who rise to the top by cruel, aggressive, belligerent methods, are wrongly regarded as strong men, and, by common standards, as mature.

If it were generally realized that such men are, in fact, extremely childish and basically incompetent to guide human affairs, the people of their nation would vote them out or overthrow them before they could do much damage. Much of the damage the 20th Century has suffered has come from men of this variety. We have them also in America. Fortunately in this country they have not been able to usurp government, but their very presence is a threat we cannot afford. It is because so many people grow up without outgrowing their hostile aggressiveness that *the only real danger of our time is man's inhumanity to man.*

Sometimes the immaturities of hostility and cruelty are displayed in full view on the surface, as they are in the gangster of the Dillinger type. That these men have their immaturity out on the surface is a fortunate thing for society, because society can and does react to it in a way appropriate to its danger. However, there are many who have the same type of immaturity but manage to keep it pretty well concealed; they are able to bring trouble to those unfortunate enough to get in their way.

The childish troublemaker. Bert, for instance, is a pleasant looking chap who would appear to be 100 per cent harmless. One of Bert's employers told me that after Bert came to his department many of his employees gradually began showing dissatisfaction and began making trouble in the department. There was a constant irritation and agitation for one thing and another. The problem became so bad that a quiet search was made for the agitator.

It turned out to be Bert, who in a quiet, pleasant, conversational sort of way dropped barbed suggestions and remarks to the other employes. Bert would put these barbs across in such a cunningly clever way that the employes themselves did not suspect that Bert was putting hostile thoughts into their heads. After Bert was fired, the department soon settled down into its old smooth ways. Bert never feels well and I suspect he never will.

Many are the women who have thrown themselves away by marrying one of these children with hair on his chest and more muscles in his arms than maturity in his head. Hell cannot hold anything worse than what these women go through on earth. Very often these husbands will have an outward bearing, appearance, and manner that make the rest of the world think well of them.

The wife will say, "Other people simply cannot appreciate how mean and cruel he is every hour he is at home."

Such fellows inevitably develop emotionally induced illness. They rightfully deserve it. But their wives do not deserve the emotional illness they get.

6. Maturity is able to distinguish fact from fancy. It is characteristic of a child to accept a fancy as a fact, and not to try to differentiate between them. A child can afford to do this almost without limit because there is usually no practical disadvantage, or advantage, in doing otherwise. However, if the child grows into responsible adulthood and still cannot distinguish between fancy and fact, the results are a terrific amount of trouble that means misery and wrong emotions.

A widespread type of childishness. It is appalling how much of this kind of immaturity exists. Someone develops an idle fancy about someone else and starts a harmful rumor which becomes accepted as a fact.

A selfish, dishonest and in-every-way-despicable politician builds up a fancy concerning his value to the republic as an enemy of totalitarianism, and a great number of honest but immature voters accept the fancy as a fact. A man takes a fancy that he hears messages from God, and persuades other people that this is a fact. Religious wars and divisive hatreds among men are started on the basis of what is actually pure nonsense. Every person I have ever known who claimed to be receiving messages from God turned out to be a schizophrenic. A childish man fancies that all human illness is due to displaced vertebrae, and gets people to accept this as fact. The communists start the fancy that their system is a heaven for the farmer and the laborer; a certain number of people accept it as fact.

With each instance of such immaturity, the world, or a part of it, must suffer. There is no immaturity that we pay for so dearly as this. It is expensive on a personal or a community level.

People who feel the world is against them. There is a common variety of this type of immaturity which especially merits attention. It is found in the individual who accepts as facts, *and worries over,* things that have never happened. Such a person lives in a terrible world of fancy, a terrible calamitous world where everything is bad, but yet a world which isn't real because it doesn't exist.

Actually, the everyday world we are in is a very enjoyable and highly interesting affair, in which the things which happen to us can be turned into some sort of a good feeling. But these immature people fancy that it is a terrible world which holds for them only the worst possible conclusions. They are afraid to stay alone in broad daylight because they accept as fact the fancy that something (they do not know what) is going to happen to them. Like the children they were and still are, they haven't grown up, and they accept as fact the fancy of their unreal fears. Such people are common patients in the doctor's office.

One patient, for instance, while working in the hay barn unloading hay, suddenly had the fancy, "Supposing there might be a snake in the hay." Now there had never been a single snake on the farm; but the fancy came; and the woman allowed her imagination to develop the fancy with many thrilling and horrible ramifications until it assumed the status of a fact in her thinking, and it became impossible for her to go to the barn.

Another lady, in her sixties, came to my office with the complaint, "I know you'll laugh at this, but I have a snake in my stomach; it's been there many months and, whenever it is irritated, it bites me and makes me miserable."

In every other respect she was perfectly sane, and, in the matter of this fancy, she was no more insane than anyone else who accepts any fancy as a fact.

You might like to hear the sequel to her snake story. No amount of examination, which included looking into her stomach with a gastroscope, could persuade the lady she had no snake. Finally one of our doctors, who was a slight-of-hand artist, contrived, while putting in and drawing out a stomach tube, to bring a garter snake out of his sleeve saying as he did so, "Well, by Jove, you did have a snake in there, and here it is."

"See," the lady said triumphantly, "I told you so all the time." She was much relieved and felt fine. Then, three months later, she came back and said, "I've got another snake in my stomach." This was in winter, and the clever slight-of-hand doctor could find no snake for his act. The patient went to another clinic with her snake before summer came. I do not know whether she still has it or not. Perhaps by this time there have been eggs and hatchings and her entire digestive tract may be full of them.

7. Flexibility and adaptability are most important parts of maturity. A person who does not learn to bend, unbroken, before a wind, and to adapt himself readily to changing conditions, cannot possibly be happy in a world where disaster can fall at any time with great rapidity and where the things we hold valuable one day entirely cease to exist the next.

Flexibility and adaptability are probably the most valuable kinds of maturity to possess. When circumstances are cruel, as they often are, when the ground we were standing on is taken from under our feet, the only quality that can stave off an illness-precipitating and misery-producing set of emotions is the ability to be flexible enough before the blows of fate to remain unbroken, and adaptable enough to carry on valiantly under the new set of conditions.

It is only by possessing this kind of maturity that a person can avoid being upset if some of his basic needs (discussed in Chapter 14) are left unfilled. Without this maturity a person is forever finding himself in trouble. One simple form of flexibility and adaptability is Pollyanna's, whose system is so good it has gone for 15 or 16 commercially-successful volumes. Her system consists in finding four good things hidden away in every bad thing that happens.

Another simple system is that of the woman who had a constantly drunken husband. She decided not to allow her situation to make her miserable, and strove to make life as pleasant as possible for herself and her children.

Another simple system is not to look back, reviewing the last catastrophe, but to look ahead, determining how much good can be introduced into the future.

➡ *Maturities and Certain Definite Attitudes*

Maturities are, after all, nothing more than certain definite attitudes we develop in regard to ourselves and our relation to our world. But they are attitudes which are not developed without learning processes. They do not come naturally to people. They are part of the things we must learn. These attitudes determine whether we live happily or unhappily, whether we live healthily, or whether we wallow in ill health.

Every person can profitably ask himself. "How mature am I? In what respects am I still immature and how can I outgrow it?" A great many people find it possible to mature after they are 30, 40, 50, or even 60. All one needs is to be shown what he needs to learn, and to have the desire to learn it.

With maturity comes emotional stasis.

IMPORTANT POINTS OF CHAPTER 7

People have emotional stress and emotionally induced illness not because of overwhelming amounts of trouble, but because they haven't learned to handle the ordinary amount of trouble which is the rule of everyone's living.

The ability to handle the various phases of ordinary human life in an effective way, that is to say, in a way that produces a maximum amount of enjoyment and a minimum amount of stress, is what is known as *maturity*.

Being *mature* means having *emotional stasis*, which is the ability to maintain equanimity, resignation, courage, determination, and cheerfulness when a situation might lead an immature person to apprehension, fear, anxiety, or frustration.

Becoming mature is a learning process. Unfortunately, there is no place today where people can learn to become mature. Our three educational institutions, the school, the church, and the family, all fall down in this essential part of our education.

Maturity consists of the following qualities:
- 1. A well grounded feeling of *responsibility* and *independence*.
- 2. A *giving* rather than a receiving attitude.
- 3. Graduating from egoism and competitiveness to *cooperativeness* and the *feeling for the human enterprise*.
- 4. Recognizing and accepting the social restrictions on sex, and making sexuality one item of many in a happy marital life.
- 5. Realizing that hostile aggressiveness, anger, hate, cruelty, and belligerency are weakness, and that *gentleness, kindness,* and *good will* are strength.
- 6. Being able to distinguish *fact* from fancy.
- 7. Being *flexible* and *adaptable* to the changes dictated by fate and fortune.

8.

HOW TO DEVELOP
EMOTIONAL STASIS

➧ *Becoming Mature Is a Grand Experience*

So we are caught, you, I, and just about everyone else, with many immaturities and emotional stress.

Really, *we* are not to blame; *we* are the victims of circumstance. The development of our maturity and our emotional stasis was educationally neglected. We have our emotional stress because of the things we didn't have a chance to learn, rather than because of the things we did learn.

This, at least, is certain: we can't go back and start constructing ourselves all over again. If we are going to improve, we'll have to start right here, in all this mess we're in, in this state of emotional confusion which to some of us seems so utterly big and heavy. There is no other way.

We've got to start improving ourselves even with all these barnacles of emotional stress hanging to us and holding us down. A fellow like me says to you, "Come on, old boy, let's improve our emotions." You look around at what looks to you like an insuperable amount of whirling, swirling, madly dashing — a tremendous amount of trouble. The invitation to develop emotional stasis in this state of affairs may look to you like an invitation to take a first swimming lesson in the lower rapids of Niagara River!

But, actually, changing over to emotional stasis and getting rid of emotional stress is simple, and what's more, *it's an exhilarating, refreshing experience*. You can begin turning immaturities into maturities almost at once.

As a matter of fact, you start today!

➤ Conscious Thought-Control

Stop just a moment to consider this interesting angle.

Suppose that the right kind of education has given lucky Henry Smith emotional stasis and maturity. Just what has this education done to Henry Smith? Principally this:

The right kind of education has trained Henry Smith to *think in certain definite ways,* and *to hold certain definite attitudes,* in the face of situations that would, in Sam Jones, who was not so trained, give rise to thoughts and attitudes producing fear, apprehension, discouragement, and similar unhealthy emotions.

In Henry Smith, who was properly trained by the right kind of education, healthy ways of thinking and healthy attitudes pop into his mind without conscious control. They just find themselves there at the right time because of the training he received.

Now here is the nubbin of the trick you and I must practice: If you and I knew just what Henry Smith's ways of thinking are, and what his attitudes are, we might, even without any educational training, bring them into our minds through conscious thought control, that is to say, *by just making them be there.*

➤ Getting on the Right Track

In other words, you are going to have to watch your thinking, just as if your Mind's Eye were standing in a little

balcony from which it can look over everything that comes
into your mind. Your Mind's Eye must watch what goes on,
and report immediately when your mind is becoming occu
pied with thinking that will generate stress.

When the report comes from your Mind's Eye that your
mind is engaged in such skulduggery, you *consciously* start
the way of thinking and *the attitude* that you might have had
if you had emotional stasis and maturity like Henry Smith.

This is a trick called *conscious thought-control.* Anyone
can do it. You can, for instance, sitting there in your chair,
direct your thoughts to your last summer's vacation or to the
vacation you are planning this summer. You can turn your
thinking in any direction you wish. Of course you can!

Now, try it. Think of something you are planning that is
really very agreeable. There, see? It's no trick at all.

The important point to know then is just *how* and *in what
direction* thought is to be controlled if we are to approximate
Henry Smith's maturity and emotional stasis. This would, at
first glance, seem like a very complex process, and it *would*
be if we had to come to a decision first as to just what Henry
Smith has that we haven't. But, fortunately, psychologists
and psychiatrists have this already prepared, cut-and-dried
for us. As a matter of fact, it has been reduced to beautifully
simple terms, readily understandable and very practical to
follow.

Now don't let me mislead you: I said *simple;* but, admittedly, following these simple directives is not always *easy,*
and there will be many times when you have to put considerable pressure behind your efforts. But since it concerns the
most important part of your personality (your maturity and
emotional stasis), and since it concerns the most important
element in your living (your happiness), and since it directly
concerns your health, *the required effort is decidedly worth
ten thousand times what it takes.*

So, let's get going. *What track is our thought control to
take?*

➡ *Here's Where You Start: The Key Thought*

The thought that you must carry all the time, like a big sign hanging over the stage of your living, is this:

**I am going to keep my thinking and my attitude calm
and cheerful right now.**

That thought you are to have always with you, repeating it over and over to yourself until it sticks there without conscious effort. Just as the present moment is always with you, so is the thought, "I am going to keep my thinking calm and cheerful — right now."

Whatever happens, whatever situation arises as the day goes along, keep that *one* thought active and alive.

And, of course, situations will arise, every day, to which you have gotten in the habit of reacting with one of the unhealthy emotions. Then you will say to yourself, "Whoa, there, old fella, here's where we need calmness and cheerfulness."

Then you must substitute a healthy emotion — one containing equanimity, courage, resignation, determination, cheerfulness and pleasantness — for that unhealthy stress emotion you might otherwise have — the one containing fear, apprehension, remorse, disappointment, anxiety, or frustration.

➡ *Substituting Healthy Emotions for Stress Emotions*

At first you'll find that you have usually *started* stewing over something, or you've already become irritated and upset before you remember to say to yourself, "I am going to keep my thinking and my attitude calm and cheerful — right now." As you practice, you'll be *ahead* of stress with the key thought, and be able to stop your descent into stressing emotions.

Either way, the moment you remember, "I am going to keep my thinking and attitude calm and cheerful — right now," you stop the thinking that generates the stress emotion and start a train of thought that will generate healthy emotions. Everybody develops his own tricks for substituting a healthy emotion for a stressing one — RIGHT NOW, when it is needed.

On the occasions that are just "nasty little situations" of minor importance, one of my patients learned to begin whistling, and soon he trilled himself into complacency, equanimity and cheerfulness. Another patient, who had a good voice and liked to sing, learned that if she sang she could change her emotions for the better at once. Another patient has learned to find beauty in the little things about her when she needs the lift. And a man told me that he keeps planning a new experience ahead that he can turn to and think about whenever he finds his emotions are running toward the stressing side.

Many people find prayer a ready way for starting a pleasant stream of emotion. But it is important to get into the prayer the same attitude of calm and cheerfulness. For instance, it would not do to pray like this: "Oh, Lord, I feel miserable, and the situation I am in is terrible. Won't you help me, God?"

The supplication should run more like this: "Thou hast created a wonderful, wonderful world for our enjoyment, O Lord. Give me the courage, the resignation, the determination, the equanimity, the cheerfulness, the pleasantness to enjoy this wonderful life Thou hast given me from Thy bounty."

These are all useful methods of substitution. They will help you out of those numerous little snarls that come along every day — the sum total of which can get you down.

➡ Mastering That Nasty Little Moment

These nasty little situations are easy to handle by remembering, "I am going to keep my thinking and my attitude calm and cheerful — *right now,*" and then deliberately call-

ing up and tossing in a healthy emotion instead of allowing
the stressing one to go ahead. It is very important in developing emotional stasis that you do handle stresses in this way.
For although each of these minor stresses may seem trivial,
yet these seemingly trivial episodes, if allowed each time to
run a stressing course, will by themselves be enough to produce chronic emotional stress and E. I. I. Eighty per cent of
the average patient's stress arises from these poorly-controlled
and relatively minor situations.

➤ If the Going Is Smooth

If you happen to be traveling through a good, smooth
period of living, then, for heaven's sake, allow yourself *to feel*
happy. Fill the hopper with equanimity, cheerfulness, and
pleasantness. Go the limit to enjoy the delightful magnificence
of your world. Life is wonderful if you allow it to be.

➤ Four Things to Do If the Going Is Rough

The big situations that may arise in your living, (you and
I have had them, and will continue to) are not as readily dealt
with as are "the nasty little moments." Suppose your wife is
sick, you can't get (in fact, you can't afford) help, the children
are at loose ends, and it looks as though your plant was about
to shut down; you already are working only three days a week.
Creditors are after you. That, my dear fellow, is not a spot
where simply substituting an emotion is going to do the trick.

There is a general mode of procedure to keep in mind:

1. First, stay outwardly as cheerful and calm as you possibly can. Lighten an awkward situation with a bit of humor,
wry though it may be. (Wry humor is, after all, the best
variety.)

2. Avoid running your misfortune through your mind
like a repeating phonograph record. Do not let yourself get
irritated, upset, or hysterical. Above all, don't start pitying
yourself.

3. Lay your plans always to turn every defeat into some kind of a victory, remembering that the best victory is to have kept your courage, your equanimity and pleasantness. Everyone will admire you for that.

4. Run these flags up on your masthead and *keep them flying:*

> Equanimity ("Let's stay calm.")
> Resignation ("Let's accept this setback gracefully.")
> Courage ("I can take this, and more.")
> Determination ("I'll turn this defeat into victory.")
> Cheerfulness ("Bowed but not broken.")
> Pleasantness ("Still good will toward men.")

➡ The Story of Two Men

You should know about these two men, and remember them as you deal with your problems. They are as different as night and day. One of them, Sam, is the perfect example of emotional stress. The other, William, is the epitome of emotional stasis.

➡ Sam, King of His Own Stew

Sam's world, if someone other than Sam inhabited it, would be a dreamland. The *only* bad feature in Sam's life is his own condition of emotional stress, which, mind you, Sam is not accountable for, since he got it through bad family education.

Sam is a well-to-do farmer and a director of a bank in a neighboring town. Sam has a wonderful farm which he inherited from his father. From his father, too, he received a grouch of the kind fairly common among "successful men." I don't think a grouch like that is inherited; it's acquired by living in the shadow of someone else's grouch. His mother was grouchy too; I imagine she got it living with Sam's father; or, perhaps, his father married the woman because she had the type of grouch he felt went with a solid citizen.

In spite of the fact that Sam had never had any hardships,

no financial losses, no extraordinary family catastrophes, no blows beneath the belt from unkind fate, he, nevertheless, walked through life as though utter and complete ruin were just around the corner.

On Sam's side of the street, the sun never shone. Sam was like the man walking in a park telling a friend how unfortunate was his every move, saying, "Some people buy bonds — they go up. Some people marry — she is a princess. For me — everything goes wrong." Just than a bird flew overhead; the complaining man took out a handkerchief and carefully cleaned a fresh spot from his lapel. "See?" he explained, "For some people they sing."

I have asked Sam's family, and Sam's neighbors, whether they have ever heard Sam say a hopeful, pleasant word, but none of them ever have. Oh, yes, I almost forgot. His wife thinks that Sam did say something pleasant the first year they were married, but that was so long ago she is no longer sure.

To illustrate how Sam's disposition operates, I drove into his farm one day in July just about the time the oats were ready to be cut. Sam had 60 acres of the nicest oats you'd ever want to see. I said, "Sam, that's a wonderful field of oats you have there." Sam answered mournfully, "Yeah, but the wind'll blow it down before I get it cut."

I watched the oats. Sam got it cut before it blew down. He got it threshed before it burned up. And I knew he received a good high price for the oats. So the next time I saw Sam I said,

"Sam, how did the oats turn out?"

"Oh, I suppose good enough," he replied, "But a crop of oats like that sure takes a lot out of the soil."

Another year he had corn that ran 165 bushels to the acre. Before it was harvested, Sam was in my office and I said, (conversationally, as well as to see whether Sam was running true to form), "How's the corn this year, Sam?"

And Sam said, "Terrible! It's so heavy I don't know how we're going to get it in."

At another time in October, I met him on the street. It was

one of those beautiful dreams of an October day that we so often have in Wisconsin. With what I thought was contagious enthusiasm I said,

"Hello, Sam. Wonderful day, isn't it?"

Sam's answer was "Yeah, but when we get it, we'll get it hard."

These outlooks are typical of Sam.

You will remember in Chapter 4 we talked about the type of emotionally induced illness that Sam has. People with Sam's emotional color *always* develop emotionally induced illness, certainly by their middle fifties. And when they get it, they get it, like Sam's weather, *hard*. Very often they are invalids for the rest of their lives.

➡ *William, King of Living*

The other man to contrast with Sam is a man still to be seen on the streets of our town. His hat is respectable but old. His coat is clean but worn. His smile is sincere; the look in his eyes is glad. He is called William.

William, too, inherited a good round sum from his father, just as Sam did. And in an adventurous sort of way he tripled it and quadrupled it, and enjoyed it, as only William knew how to enjoy.

Then came 1929 and 1930. The bankers (and one was particularly bad) set upon William gleefully, and cleaned him out. I am told, on good authority, that with a little lenience William could have come through the depression in good condition. But this one banker snapped up what William had, while the snapping was good. William went on W.P.A.

I stopped one day when I saw him digging in a ditch with a string of other men. William was 60, and he hadn't worked at manual labor for years, if ever. When he saw me he smiled a great big smile and rested on his shovel.

"You might almost say," he laughed, "that you are watching an honest man earn an honest dollar. But it isn't quite true. I earn only 79 cents of it. The rest of the time I lean on my shovel and talk. But then that's what the Government wants — it's not so much to get this ditch dug as it is to help the public's morale, and so the 21 cents I don't earn shoveling, I make up for by boosting the general morale of these fellows working here with me."

All the fellows down in the ditch laughed with him. They had been feeling good ever since he joined them. He always made everybody feel good.

William still had a few irons in the fire and he made a little money over and above his W.P.A. intake. But then both he and his wife, whom he adored, developed an abdominal malignancy at the same time.

Each had an operation. He lived and was cured. But he lost his wife. And it took all his recent savings to pay the hospital. Through the whole thing, William never changed; he never talked about himself, nor complained.

He had a pleasant story, an interesting anecdote, cheerful greetings, whenever anyone came to see him in his hospital room. His wife's death must have made a great hole in his life, but he never let on. He filled it with the old smile which shone now beneath the battered hat that was all he could afford. Here and there, he made a little to live on, one way and another, but always happy.

Then he developed a malignancy of the larynx. More operations. I'd see him in the office, and he had so many interesting things to tell me I had difficulty finding out how *he* was. And, miraculously, he was cured of the malignancy in his larynx. He still goes around the town, smiling, interested in everything, and interesting everyone in something.

Probably the most remarkable thing about William is this: The banker who cleaned William out in the depression has never had a friend. I have never heard anyone say a good or kind word about him — except William.

William thinks the banker is a man of great capacity, and told me once, "People think the man has no heart, but he is kind, really. Nobody seems to pay any attention when he is kind, but they sure talk about it when he does the kind of thing a banker necessarily has to do."

One of William's neighbors, having admired the manner in which Will kept his head up, the cheerful smile on his lips, and the friendly, unwhining greeting through all his misfortune, stopped Will one morning and said, "William, if you'll excuse me, I want to say simply that I admire the way you come through misfortune after misfortune. I'd sure like to know your recipe. Would you mind giving it to me?"

William smiled warmly. Like everyone else, he liked a pat on the back.

"Well, I'll tell you. A long time ago I sat down to try to figure out my next move. It didn't look as though there was another move. I thought a long time. And then the answer came to me. I got up and repeated it to myself, 'William, you might just as well cooperate with the inevitable.' And that's what I've been doing ever since — cooperating with the inevitable."

➡ The Importance of Handling the Average Moment

Let me give you one more example of the general procedure for you to follow, this time an example of how to handle, and how not to handle, the "nasty little moment."

Some time ago, I chanced to go Christmas shopping with two ladies in the department stores of Chicago. These two ladies were twin sisters.

The first of these sisters had left a chronically-ill husband at home, and had a boy fighting in the Far East. The second sister had nothing in her life to cause a ripple.

The first sister knew the art of enjoyment, that is to say, she knew how to attain emotional stasis. She made herself enjoy the entire day.

When we went into a department store, she would look around at the holiday decorations in genuine pleasure and say something like, "I just love to shop at Christmas, the stores are all so gay."

If we stopped at a counter looking for some particular article, she would exclaim with pleasure, "My, they have such a wonderfully rich selection of everything. I've got a better choice of better things right here than any Roman Empress ever had," or, "Oh, wouldn't Charles just be thrilled to death with this? Why it just suits him to a T."

We had lunch in a department store restaurant. She said as we entered, "I always like to eat in here, it's so nice and big, and the meals are always so delicious." She enjoyed the whole meal, and we started out again with a neat tip to the waitress.

Her sister, on the other hand, had no reason for acting differently, except her acquired habit.

As we entered a store — the very same store — she looked around in horror, "Just look at all the crowds. I just hate to do Christmas shopping."

At a counter she would say, "They have so much you just don't know what to choose. They simply have too much. Last year the thing I got Charley he didn't like, and I know he wouldn't like this either. And look at the prices. It's positively robbery, that's what it is."

In the department store restaurant, nothing was right or satisfactory. She complained to the waiter of every bit of food that came before her, and finally she became irritated because the waitress reached in front of her. She made a scene with the manager that I thought would never be over. She entirely spoiled her own meal, and she could have spoiled her sister's and mine if we had not (knowing her) found her intensely amusing.

The next day the pleasant twin felt fine and chipper, and was about her usual work. But the self-made battle-ax was sick abed with a migraine headache, as I knew she would be. "Why in the world," she grumbled belligerently, "do I get these headaches? Oh, oh, I'm so sick."

A SUMMARY OF THE AIDS
FOR DEVELOPING EMOTIONAL STASIS
PRESENTED IN CHAPTER 8

I. Practice thought control. When you catch yourself starting a stressing emotion like worry, anxiety, fear, apprehension, or discouragement, *STOP IT*. Substitute a healthy emotion like equanimity, courage, determination, resignation, or cheerfulness.

II. Carry this idea every minute of every day: *I am going to keep my attitude and thinking calm and cheerful — right now.*

III. When the going is good and smooth, allow yourself the delightful feeling of being happy.

IV. When the going gets rough:

1. Stay outwardly as cheerful and as pleasant as you possibly can. Lighten an awkward situation with a bit of humor, wry though it may be.

2. Avoid running your misfortune through your mind like a repeating phonograph record. Above all, do not let yourself get irritated, upset, or hysterical.

3. Try to turn every defeat into a moral victory.

4. Run these flags up on your masthead and *keep them flying:*

* *Equanimity* ("Let's stay calm.")
* *Resignation* ("Let's accept this setback gracefully.")
* *Courage* ("I can take all this and more.")
* *Determination* ("I'll turn this defeat into victory.")
* *Cheerfulness* ("Really, I'm holding my own," or, "Bowed but not broken.")
* *Pleasantness* ("I'll still have good will toward men.")

9.

TWELVE IMPORTANT PRINCIPLES TO MAKE YOUR LIFE RICHER

Your maturity and emotional stasis will take a great step forward if you can maintain certain attitudes toward several of the important broad aspects of living. These all involve departments of living that seem to give many people considerable trouble, departments of living in which people are apt to react with typical immaturity and develop much emotional stress.

It is best to formulate a definite mature plan of action in handling these aspects of life that cause people so much stress. Let us examine such guiding principles. They will save you an immeasurable amount of stress.

➧ 1. *Keep Life Simple*

Keep yourself responsive to the simple things that are always near at hand and readily accessible. Don't get in the habit of requiring the *unusual* for your pleasure, a failing one is very likely to find in people having more than a little money or education.

Life becomes a tremendously interesting adventure if you learn how to get your pleasures from the world that lies immediately before your five senses.

How easy and simple it is to live enjoyably when the simple, interminable blue of the sky, with its long wisps of white cloud, becomes a pleasant thing to behold, a thing of beauty that thrills you every time you care to look skyward. How easy to live when the grain in the panelling of the door arouses your admiration, or a scrambled egg satisfies, or plain Mrs. What's-her-name down the street becomes an object of keen interest because of her absorbing preoccupation with her lawn.

How simple and how nice to live like Gilbert White of Selbourne, like W. C. English, John Muir, or Thoreau, occupied with the constant, wonderful world of color, sound, smell, and sight that is available every single instant. If you tune yourself to it as Walt Whitman did, your every moment is a walk down an avenue of ready-made enjoyment.

W. C. English, a remarkable man. One of the finest men it has been my great fortune to know was a man who made himself entirely happy in the world that lies at the tips of our fingers, visible to our immediate sight, and always within hearing. His name was W. C. English.

I met him when I was in college; he was already in his sixties. W. C. English was John Burroughs, John Muir, and Gilbert White of Selbourne all rolled into one. He enjoyed everything around him. His life was simple, his only needs were eyes to see, ears to hear, nose to smell, and fingers to feel.

He needed no automobile to travel. He could see more afoot. And in a mile afoot, he found infinitely more wonder than most people find in ten thousand miles on wheels. He knew every plant, every bush, every tree, by its scientific name, as well as its common name. He knew the places where the pink lady's-slipper grew, where to find the fringed avens. He knew what plants the Indians used for food, for paint, for other purposes; he knew how to prepare them. The few people who have eaten one of his meals of wild Indian vegetables beside an oak fire on the bluffs of the Wisconsin River have had one of the rare experiences men can have.

He knew the insects. They astounded him. Through personal observation he knew the life histories of some insects that were known to no other man. He enjoyed the birds and could spot and name them from far off. The Wisconsin River Valley he knew as no other man has known it. He thoroughly knew his world, and was entirely at home in it. At night he was at home with the stars and the sounds of the forest.

He showed me how to catch sight of a wild deer, where to find the badger, how to trick a fox into showing where he lived, where to expect a rattlesnake and how to pick him up. He knew about geology, fossils, and caves.

In all this, he was not a pedant, but just a smiling, pleasant man with his hat tipped back on his head, striding along easily with long strides, enjoying a world in which *everything* interested him.

I have seen him spend a whole afternoon watching a jumping spider. He lectured when he needed money, or wrote an article. But he had no great need for money, because he was richer than Henry Ford and John D. Rockefeller combined. He would chuckle when he heard of other people's misfortunes, asking why people should be foolish enough to cause themselves so much trouble. For him the people he met were as interesting as the plants and birds, and he treated them with the same solicitude.

He was one man who was truly loved and respected by all who knew him. His wife always said that she adored him more every year. They lived 60 years together.

We can't, of course, be W. C. English's, or live like him. But the point is, we should cultivate the ability to find our major and constant enjoyments in the common things which are always at hand. To be able to do so gives living a most tremendous lift whose value cannot be overestimated. Developing a capacity for enjoying what is at hand, of course, carries with it simplicity in living.

Now, mind you, it doesn't preclude soaring into the heights, but it makes soaring what it is, namely, a *soaring,* after which one again returns to set one's feet on the terra firma of the world of our five senses, rather than making soaring a permanently insecure detachment from which there is no return because there is no place to return to.

➤ 2. *Avoid Watching for a Knock in Your Motor*

Among the world's most miserable people are those who cannot get over the idea that they have something terribly and intrinsically wrong somewhere — something very rotten in the state of their constitutions. They are forever miserable, listening for a possible knock in their motors, a grinding in their differentials. They belong to a tremendously large organization — the "Symptom-a-Day-Club," in which it is required that the members start the day by waking up and immediately asking themselves, "Where am I sick today?"

Bellyachers are miserable people deserving our greatest sympathy and help. They have gotten the way they are because of:

(1) *Parents who were chronic bellyachers,* and who gave their poor miserable children the idea that our bodies are hellholes of aches, pains, and agues.

(2) *Doctors who gave them an organic substitute explanation for their E. I. I.* These doctors were either inexperienced or were thinking more of their fee or their time, than they were of the patient.

(3) *An interesting physiological fact*: if any of us stop and ask ourselves, "Where do I hurt?" we can by self-examination find some place where we hurt. The bellyacher by habitual self-examination is constantly finding these places and playing them for all they are worth. All one needs to do to turn one of these insignificant, unimportant pains into something genuinely severe is to keep one's attention on the pain. It soon grows ten times as severe.

A common fuel for the bellyacher's fire is a common type

of muscle-sheath and tendon pain known as fibrositis. Fibrositis *never* turns into anything serious. Although it is primarily an emotionally induced symptom, it is aggravated by muscular exertion, and by temperature and moisture changes. It is exceedingly common, and there are few people who do not have it.

Some people, like myself, have fibrositis somewhere practically all the time. The bellyachers manage to squeeze every ounce of pain out of their fibrositis. Not knowing that it is *merely* fibrositis, they add apprehension to it; if the fibrositis is in the chest, they are sure they have heart trouble; if it is in their scalp, they have a brain tumor; if it is in the abdomen, they have the cancer that is the beginning of the end.

Sometime when you haven't anything else to do (God help you), center your awareness for an hour on the sensations that arise in your throat. At the end of the hour you will understand how a person who has allowed himself the apprehension that there is something wrong with his throat can feel so sure that his throat is plugged, swollen, inflamed, dripping, abscessed, cancerous — in short, fulminatingly catastrophic — beyond anything the medical profession has ever witnessed before. What a sneering look of contempt the M.D. receives who assures such a throat searcher that he has nothing wrong with his throat!

There are a terrific number of people, physiologically sound but emotionally unsound, who have developed the idea they are unwell, and who no more expect to be well in the future than you and I expect to grow younger. Sad to say, in the development of this idea they have often been ably abetted by some lazy physician who offered them an easy organic explanation for feeling the way they do.

For instance, I had as a patient a lady who was sure she had some unusual fluid trickling about in odd ways in her abdomen. She had already had three major operations. She had a small myoma of the uterus that actually amounted to exactly nothing.

She had been told by a surgically-minded physician that the

myoma was the cause of her trouble and should be taken out. I thought I was doing pretty well in allaying her fears and explaining her feelings. Then, in a moment of doubt, she returned to the surgically-minded individual of the first part.

He operated, assuring her afterward that not only had he removed the offending uterus, but that, through his magnanimity, her ovaries, too, would never after cause her any trouble. She felt well and was fairly happy for two months. Then she had a new set of complaints.

Now her thinking was, "If my former trouble was caused by *something* that had to be removed, this one is, too." Now rational treatment is even more difficult than it was before. I am trying again, but I'm afraid the idea is pretty well fixed in her mind that she has a diseased organ again, and is never to be well. *She never expects to be well.* She is a sitting duck for the next physician who suggests an operation.

But it isn't always the doctor's fault. Josephine was a pretty maiden lady who was sacrificing herself to take care of her mother and father. The plans she had once made for her own adventure in living had been laid aside. On the surface she appeared pleasant enough, but, fundamentally, she rebelled secretly against her lot.

She had an ulcer, and she centered all her complaints around that. Her complaints, and her parents' complaints, became so wearing that her physician consented to an operation for her ulcer. Now, several years later, she is just as miserable abdominally as she was before, this time without an ulcer. The physician was literally pushed into an operation. He knew he could remove her ulcer, but he also knew he couldn't remove the situation that would produce new abdominal difficulties after the ulcer was removed.

Never before in history have people been bombarded by so many warnings of ill health as we are today. The radio and television are constantly suggesting symptoms in order to sell a remedy which even the truly sick do not need. Anyone in a properly receptive mental state can feel the necessary symptoms and buy a bottle of the stuff the commercial on the radio or television makes so alluringly curative. Daily papers and magazines whoop up a disease and recite enough average feelings as symptoms, so that anyone can imagine he has the disease, or that he soon will have it. Never before in history has a public been made so aware and so afraid of the diseases which our clay is heir to. This constitutes a tremendous factor in the onset of emotionally induced illness.

A person may have symptoms from wrong emotions. If he pays no attention to these symptoms, either because he knows what they are, or because he has other more important things to think about, he cannot be said to have emotionally induced illness. But the moment he gets apprehensive, and concerned, about the symptoms he feels, and allows them to make him miserable, he has emotionally induced illness.

One of my patients was an executive of a large concern. He was always under terrific pressure, with large responsibilities. As he went about his work, he frequently felt a tightness in his chest, and because it was not actually uncomfortable, and because he was intent on his job, he paid no attention to it but went on his way.

During a routine physical examination he mentioned the tightness to the company doctor, who told the executive that he probably had early coronary heart disease. From then on the poor fellow was licked; he thought of his heart all the time, and became extremely apprehensive whenever the tightness appeared. He became unable to work and was a complete invalid for a year. It took numerous examinations by the best heart specialists in the country, and very intensive assurative therapy, to get the man back to his work. Finally, he could again evaluate the tightness for what it was — a manifestation of the harrying and worrying, anxiety and hurrying, that was a part of his job.

But be sure you are organically sound. Here is the way to take care of your health. Have a good thorough physical examination every year by a sensible doctor, to assure yourself that you are sound, or practically sound. Between the yearly examinations *believe* you *are* sound. If something turns up to cast any doubt in your mind as to your condition, go to the same doctor. If your fear turns out to be groundless (as fears usually do) make nothing further of it. It is so much more enjoyable to know that you are well than to believe there must be something morbidly wrong with you in spite of what the doctor says.

We saw in Part I how a constant, morbid fear that there must be something wrong will eventually produce E. I. I.

➤ 3. *Learn to Like Work*

The chances are that you, like most of the rest of us, have to work for a living. As with every other necessary factor in your life, you might just as well like it and avoid making trouble for yourself by not liking it.

A person who has convinced himself that he doesn't like work has a monotonous repetition of unpleasant emotions while he is working, and he is well on the way to an E. I. I. There was a time when I used to suggest to a person who didn't like the type of work he was doing that he find himself a job he did like. But I found that usually such a person didn't like the second job any better than the first. The root of the matter was that he just didn't like WORK — period.

It is perfectly obvious that anyone not liking work will have a dreadful set of emotions while he is working. And, as is usual with such people, they intermittently find an excuse for not working. Then the economic pressures that go with no income produce an even more dreadful set of emotions.

The loafer is not the happy man. There has long been a myth, half-believed in every generation for centuries, to the effect that the lazy loafer is a happy person. A happy, lazy loafer is such an outstanding envy to the folks who slave for a living that he draws a great deal more comment than most human beings do, and more than he is entitled to. But he is, nevertheless, a very definite exception to the rule. The rule is that most lazy loafers are miserable people. Of 25 lazy loafers I know personally, only one is outstandingly carefree and happy. And he happens to be a very energetic man; he is merely energetic in unproductive ways.

Unless, then, you expect to end up either in prison or on relief, you had better persuade yourself that you like work. Dislike for work carries with it unpleasant emotions in more ways than one.

We have our likes and dislikes because they were suggested to us, sometimes boldly and outright, sometimes insidiously and slyly. It is very easy, especially if you are still young and not too strongly set in your ways, to keep suggesting to yourself that you *like* work. The stronger and more frequent the suggestion, the better the "take." After a little practice, you can get up in the morning, pound your fists on your chest, like Tarzan, and yell, "Come on, work! Bring on the work!"

A young person in high school or in college is often desperately troubled and bothered about what kind of work he should choose, or what kind he is most adapted to. Actually what choice he makes is not very important. Any person can do a number of things equally well; some people could succeed in any kind of work. The important ingredient is that the individual *wants* to work. With that one quality, he will make a good doctor, a good plumber, or a good teacher. Without it, he won't be worth having around at any kind of a job. What's more, he will be a drug to himself.

If a person likes to work, and has learned the simple joy of doing something well, if he feels pleased at producing something of value to society, he will be generating pleasant emotions for himself all the time he is working, as well as for the chap who hires him.

A person who has more than enough work to keep himself occupied, and who likes work, seldom develops E. I. I. He does not have time to "think." "Thinking" usually means thumbing mentally over troubles. I mentioned earlier in this book that the group in my local society who have E. I. I. least often are the farmers' wives who have eight or nine children,

who take care of their homes, and also work on the farm.
They don't have time to "think" or to get sick. As one patient,
who had too little to do, put it, "I'm all right until I start
to think."

Work is therapy. Liking to work is a wonderful prophy-
laxis against E. I. I.

▶ 4. Have a Good Hobby

A fascinating and creative interest apart from your work
is an absolute essential for happy living. Two of our basic
needs are the needs for new experiences and for creative
effort. A good hobby supplies them both.

Without a hobby, spare time becomes a boring span of
time during which our minds are more and more apt to
cogitate upon our troubles.

There are any number of interesting and creative hobbies;
I do not have to name them for you. On the whole, I would
say that the creative hobbies are more satisfactory than the
collecting hobbies. But collecting hobbies are not bad.

I remember one patient, a lady in her early seventies, who
for 40 years had carried on a monologue of how miserable
her abdomen felt. She could occupy hours telling the miserable stories of her visits to the country's greatest doctors;
what each did, what each said, what each tried, and how her
abdomen emerged victorious each time and continued un-
improved or even worse than it had been. There were em-
bellishments and details which varied a bit with each re-
counting, but even these became old and worn to the immediate family, who were tired of the tale and probably tired
of seeing the raconteur live on to tell it yet again. Her children avoided her to avoid hearing the story *ad nauseam*. She
added their alienation to the current chapters of her miserable
saga.

On one visit, as I listened to her extended story, as I had
listened many times before, I managed to get a word in edge-
wise, saying, "Why don't you get yourself a hobby?"

I received no answer at the time — she went right on into her transverse colon and all the mischief that lay therein. But to my surprise, she called up two weeks later on the telephone and said, "I've got a hobby."

"Good," I answered, "What is it?"

"Button collecting," she replied.

My immediate feeling was, "Oh, pshaw — button collecting!" But since then, I have watched her collect buttons, and I think I'll take it up myself sometime. It has done the intestinal lady a world of good. In fact, it has made a likeable lady out of her.

Now when she hears about a certain button, she will go out searching for it — perhaps, the search may take many days. When she finds the button, she puts it on a card with similar buttons and puts the card up on the living room wall. Now when visitors come to see her, she actually finds it more to her liking to tell them the stories of the buttons than the story of her miserable bowel. Her family is drifting back, interested, also, in the buttons.

One day the lady went to Madison to see the Governor of Wisconsin, at that time Governor Goodland. He was 84 years old, she 74. When she had been admitted to the Governor's presence, she said, "I've come, Governor, to ask you for a button from your vest to put in my button collection."

"I'll be glad to give you one," the Governor replied, "But I haven't anything to cut a button off with."

The lady had foreseen that difficulty. She promptly extracted a pair of scissors from her handbag and handed it to the Governor. That worthy man proceeded to cut all the buttons from his vest and all the buttons from his coat.

As he handed them to the lady he said, "There you are, madam. I'd give you more, but I have to get home."

➡ 5. *Learn to Be Satisfied*

There is one understandable excuse for being dissatisfied: when there is obvious negligence, dishonesty, carelessness, or incompetence on someone's part, for example, your Congressman's. But it is obviously *useless* to be dissatisfied when a situation cannot be altered, or when dissatisfaction can be seen to be entirely useless.

For instance, you meet people who are obviously disturbed by the weather and, just as easily, by everything else. Living in chronic dissatisfaction is about as close to living in Hell as anything the world has to offer. The real tragedy is that it is so useless and unnecessary.

You remember the twin sisters I went Christmas shopping with. The one found it just as easy, and much more pleasant, to be satisfied with all the things her sister found it necessary to be dissatisfied with.

This habit of dissatisfaction is often acquired innocently by a child living in a family where one or both parents are continually at odds with everyone and everything else.

Other people acquire the habit of dissatisfaction in a different way. Albert was a boy who was awkward and "queer." The other children loved to use him as a scapegoat for their cruelty. Albert gradually came to suspect and dislike all other people. He came to dislike things other people liked or thought important. Today he registers dissatisfaction with everything and everyone, excepting himself, whom he is unconsciously defending in everything he does and thinks.

A few others become habitually dissatisfied because a series of misfortunes has soured them on everything, and they weren't originally equipped with the fortitude to rise above it. This kind of thing is apt to happen to the man or woman who picks a lemon in marriage and then has to live with it. There are so many people attached, really tragically attached, to marital lemons that it is a great credit to *homo sapiens* that so few murders are actually committed. Henry once told me the secret, and Henry knew, for he was irrevocably riveted to about the sourest lemon I ever saw. Well, the secret, Henry said, was to cultivate a taste for lemons.

If I ever have enough money to erect a statue to anyone, it will be a statue for Henry. Henry, through 33 horrible years, took a terrible, unmerciful beating; while he took it, he maintained a cheerful disposition, a warm, friendly out-look on the world and an unusual degree of good will toward men. There have been saints who were not half so deserving. And many men like Henry are flowers born to blush unseen, and waste their sweetness on the desert air. I hope someday I can raise enough money for a statue, or a sculptured group to praise them all.

A classic example of dissatisfaction. A young lady patient of mine had to be hospitalized with emotionally induced ill-ness. She was a mess. Her underlying trouble was that she had become thoroughly dissatisfied with *everything* in her life. She had been educated in an excellent eastern school to be a secretary and had a wonderful position in Washington, D. C., when World War II came along and brought a certain young, handsome army captain in and out of the office in which she worked.

One and one add up to four — I mean two, at first — they were married and had two children by the time the war was over, over, that is, for everyone but Ellen. Then she found herself living in a trailer, bringing up her children in a trailer (soon there were three).

The first time I was called to see her, she was in bed at one end of the trailer, and the captain stood wringing his hands at the other end. She told me then, in no uncertain terms, and in a voice that made the captain's fingers white, that she didn't like housekeeping "A-tall," AND she didn't like living in a TRAILER, OR keeping house in a TRAILER, AND bringing up children in a TRAILER was TERRIBLE, AND (this she didn't say, but implied) she wasn't sure she liked her husband in a TRAILER — AND she CERTAINLY wished she had stuck to her secretary's job in Washington.

I was sure, from other remarks, she was dissatisfied with her physician since he wasn't getting her over her nausea and dizziness. She welcomed the idea of the hospital for the simple reason it took her out of that so-and-so trailer. Without giving her a diagnosis, I *ordered* her (we were past the suggesting stage) to send to the library for the four Pollyanna books they had.

Now, many people may consider them silly books, but usually the people who call them silly are on the defensive because of a rotten disposition, and they half-way know it. Anyway, the young lady read the books. I didn't say a thing; at the moment, she was enjoying the hospital.

One morning she volunteered her own diagnosis. I had known all along she was bright enough. She said, "I've been thinking, or trying to think. Good Lord, what a little fool I am. I've been dissatisfied with keeping house; I've been dissatisfied at having to bring up children in a trailer; I've been dissatisfied with my husband because he couldn't provide something better; I've been dissatisfied because I'm not a secretary with a good job.

"All right, Doc, I've been thinking — I'm a damn fool. I can't change this, at least not right away. You and Pollyanna win; what am I making myself miserable for? Here's the answer: Keeping house in a trailer is, after all, very easy and no trick at all. If Jud and I don't like the view out of our living room window, we can move the trailer and get a better view.

"As for bringing up children in a trailer, there is a great expanse of outdoors for them to run around in, and you don't get that on 33d Street. I'm going to make a go of it, and I'm going to start planning a little house, the kind Jud and I want some day. AND — bless me — I wouldn't trade this for the best secretarial job in the world."

You see, *she had the idea, the simple idea, that it's easier to be satisfied than dissatisfied, and much healthier.* She read all the Pollyanna books — I guess there must be about 16. She quickly learned the art of being satisfied. She evolved her own little mental tricks and had a lot of fun doing it. It wasn't long before she was perfectly well.

As I say she really had a great deal of good sense. She soon found happiness in her family. Finally they moved into the house she and Jud had dreamed of. I like to visit them to see how pleasant and cheerful a family can be when they understand how important it is to stay that way.

It's not hard to feel good. In regard to satisfaction and dissatisfaction, remember two things:

First, it is as easy, and much pleasanter, to find elements of satisfaction instead of dissatisfaction in the daily run of events. All that is required is *the will* to feel satisfied. The wise individual knows that life is one damned frustration after another if you allow yourself to be frustrated, but it is also one satisfaction after another if you are determined to be satisfied. *Trouble is where you make it.*

Don't want what you can't have. Secondly, another trick for dispelling dissatisfaction is to quit *wanting*, wanting this, wanting that. This, of course, goes back to our first aid, which was cultivating the simple and the things at hand. I knew a man of moderate means with a large family, who made himself miserable wanting things he couldn't afford. First, he longed for an expensive camera. He worked himself into such an irritation of desire that he finally bought it, although he could ill afford it, and his family could afford it even less. When he had that, he began to fairly itch for a power saw and could think of little else until he had that; next, he had to have a drill press. And so it went on. He was always dissatisfied with what he had and thought he needed more. His family, meanwhile, were deprived of much they really needed.

It would have been just as easy for this man to have found pleasure in things that it was easier for him to have. His education had been faulty; there had been no one to show him how to find enjoyment without expense. With a little help he might have learned to enjoy the beauties and wonders which surround us on all sides. Had he invested a dollar for a copy of Gilbert White's, *The Natural History of Selbourne*, he would have found there is more in a simple walk than in a houseful of gadgets.

Learning the trick of being satisfied goes a long way toward making us well-adjusted, efficient, happy, and the possessors of a rich and rewarding life.

➡ 6. *Like People and Join the Human Enterprise*

In a world where people live next door to each other, rub elbows in the subway, and meet bumper-to-bumper on the highways, it is disastrous to emotional stasis to take a dislike to the race and to the individuals who comprise it. Letting people get in your hair is far, far worse than getting bats in it. There are many more people than bats.

Some people dislike everybody. It is surprising in meeting people with E. I. I. how many people there are in the world who dislike practically everyone, from the president, whom they have never met, to their next-door neighbor, whom they wish they had never met! They have nothing complimentary to say about a single soul, and are very derogatory toward everyone. Their immaturity has isolated them in a shell. Yet they *have* to live in the world of people. The extent of their cooperation in the affairs of people consists in getting what *they* require out of society.

One of my patients was a man who had risen to be the superintendent of a manufacturing plant employing six thousand people. He was sick. In the beginning of his illness, he would suddenly be overcome by a spell of weakness, trembling, dizziness, and vomiting. This occurred whenever he went to his office, which he shared with the other assistant manager. These spells became more and more frequent, and, before long, he began having them at home whenever he merely thought about his office. Naturally he lost weight, and both he and his wife were quite certain that he had some serious malignancy and his days were numbered.

The root of his trouble was that he didn't like the other assistant manager who occupied the same office with him. He said, "The first time I saw him, I didn't like him. I didn't like the way he combed his hair. I didn't like the way he whistled through his teeth, and the way he always started every sentence with the word 'listen,' and ended every paragraph with 'don't you know.'"

On questioning him further, I learned that he had never liked anyone. He hadn't liked his father, his mother, his brothers and sisters. He couldn't say that he cared for his wife. In short, he had never liked anyone.

He was a surprised man to find that he recovered from his illness when he began to suggest to himself the things he could find likeable about the man he had to work with, to assure himself that this man had likeable qualities, and to take the trouble to cultivate him and take him out for a round of beers.

Most people's peeves are an expression of their dislike for other people. I asked one of my patients to write down a list of his peeves, since he seemed to have so many. He filled out both sides of a sheet of typewriter-sized paper.

The first peeve he listed was "people chewing gum." "I can't stand anybody chewing gum," he said. "It just makes me grit my teeth." His second peeve was, "My wife rocking in a rocking chair. I just want to jump up and down and scream when she does that." His third peeve was, "My daughter playing the piano." And so on, and on. You can imagine how miserable his peeves must have made his family.

These dislikes are essentially childish. Dislikes like this are childish arrests in the selfish, self-centered attitude typical of childhood. Because people so afflicted are in their shell, they either never make friends or they drop the friends they start to make. This they blame not on themselves (Heaven forbid) but on the other people, whom they regard as being incapable of friendship. Next, on finding themselves isolated, they begin to pity themselves and to feel persecuted. They become hypochondriacal and develop deep-seated inferiorities. In all these ways, in addition to the plain irritations which other people cause them, these individuals lead a miserable life.

One of the finest sides to living is liking people and wanting to share actively in the human enterprise, the sum total of the effort the human race is making to get out of the jungle state and frame of mind. The greatest pleasures come by giving pleasure, to the fellow who works with us, to the chap who lives next door, or to those who live under the same roof.

There is no such thing as an "individual" in our society. Each one of us is an "individual-community." If everyone in the United States were to begin today to live entirely as an individual without the materials and services he receives from the community (the people around him) there wouldn't be more than a couple of hundred people alive at the end of a year.

Entering consciously into this human enterprise, feeling one's self a part of the community, and looking upon one's self as an "individual-community" is an important element in maturity.

➡ 7. *Get the Habit of Saying the Cheerful, Pleasant Thing*

There are some people, like Sam, who have never been heard to utter anything but a jarring note. Such a note ruins the present moment; a steady stream of them turns the whole day into a junk pile. Some people do it regularly; usually one hears it from the very high and the very low. The very low think they ought to gripe, so they gripe. The very high think they should sound worthy of their position, so they gripe at the taxes and the political opposition; they lambaste everyone under them.

Hardly a moment arises during an entire lifetime that wouldn't benefit more by a sally of humor or a cheerful lift than by a mean barb or a sharp gripe. I know executives who carry on under tremendous pressure as affably and kindly as a girl skipping down the street. They are the boys who get along and stay out of the hospitals.

On the other hand, there is the great-tycoon variety. They snarl and hiss and backfire, slugging everybody verbally — in short, making constant, ugly asses of themselves. You do not have to envy this great tycoon type, gentle reader, this constantly enraged bull who paws and bellows. You may be sure he is feeling just as miserable as he sounds. In his climb up the ladder of success, he is just as miserable on the top rung as he was on the bottom rung. The added difference is that on the top rung he is dizzy with his own eminence, and that starts another immature rush of emotions that gives him, as well as those around him, a pain in the neck.

Get up on the right side of the bed. Get the habit of starting out the day right. A neat little trick is to look at your husband, or your wife, when you are both awake, and, even if it is an overstatement, say, "Good-morning, dear; you look fine this morning."

The next neat little trick is to go to the window, look out, and in a beautiful baritone, or soprano, that reaches to the end of the avenue, sing, "Oh, What a Beautiful Morning." Should it be raining, you say enthusiastically, "Ah, what a fine rain. Certainly good for the soil."

Sounds a bit silly, of course, but it pays off. Positively the easiest way to lift your mind out of the mud is to dash off a series of pleasant remarks, or still better, a good funny story. The more adept you become in pleasantries, cheerios, and humor, the easier it is to stay out of despondency, frustration, and E. I. I. Incidentally, good humor is a quality which endears you to other people. No one loves a crepehanger. Everyone likes to have someone around who has a sense of pleasantness and humor.

Be pleasant to your family. It is particularly important in family life to develop the habit of pleasant conversation when the family is together. Do not, for your own, your children's, or your digestion's sake, make the family meal a recitation of troubles, anxieties, fears, warnings, and accusations. And what is more important, don't let the feeling pervade your family that everyone is so taken for granted that a pleasantness or kind word is unnecessary. The crabbed note that clangs daily in so many families is a good foundation for many of the neurotic characteristics of later life.

A sense of humor is a wonderful adjunct to common sense. There are various degrees and varieties. Practically everyone can develop a sense of humor if he goes after it.

One of our town's clergymen was about as humorless as a dried apricot. Moreover, it was very difficult for him to engage people in a conversation. He gradually overcame both defeats in this way: every day he read a good story and memorized it. The next day he would tell his story to everyone he met. Every day he would do the same. Usually the person to whom he told his story gave one in return. Gradually he came to recognize a good story when he heard one, and gradually he could pull a story out of his bag for almost any occasion. He became known around the country as the clergyman with the good story. People were happy to see him approach.

➡ 8. *Meet Adversity by Turning Defeat into Victory*

Many people are precipitated into E. I. I. by some adversity. Everything they had appears at one moment to have vanished, and they are completely at a loss to go on. Futility and frustration are piled on disaster. The underlying crack in most of the people who give way beneath adversity is the immaturity of selfishness and egocentricity. The death of a person near to them is calculated in terms of what it means to them, personally, in the way of services lost.

One poor woman who had always been highly selfish and self-centered became hysterical after her husband died, to the point where she insisted that her son withdraw permanently from college to keep her company. "Otherwise, I'll be alone here! I can't be all alone! I've got to have someone here!" and so on. No real thought or kindness for the man who had passed away, or for the son whose life she was continuing to ruin.

Do you remember William — King of Living — we talked about in chapter 8? At the time his wife died of a malignant disease of the intestines, he was in the hospital convalescing from an operation for the same thing. No married couple had ever been more firmly attached to one another, nor more appreciative of each other's company than Mr. and Mrs. William had been.

He took the news of his wife's death thoughtfully. He considered it silently for a few minutes. Then in a very appreciative, straightforward tone, he began to tell of incidents which illustrated what a remarkable and fine person his wife had been. After that he never referred to her or her death. He never bemoaned the fact that now he would be all alone. When he left the hospital to return to his two rooms, in which he was now to be alone, he did so without a mention that it would be changed or that the rooms they had called "home" would be without the presence of his wife.

When I called on him there, he was just the same as before; he was just as cheerful, he was just as interested in the great wide world as he had ever been. He never dropped a note to indicate that his life was different now, or empty. Soon he was out and around, talking to old friends (and everyone is his friend), apparently unperturbed.

A few years later I met him on the street outside my office. "Well, howdy, Doctor," he said, "You look as though you had to get somewhere fast."

"No," I replied, "No hurry, just a habit. I'm on my way to see a type of patient one always hates to see — a woman who has been upset and in bed ever since her husband died four months ago." Then I added that few people were able to handle adversity the way he could.

"It isn't hard to do," he said, "if you keep your feet where they belong — on the ground. When you can't change something — you'd better accept it, and figure out how you can keep living the best possible way. When a man loses his wife, or a wife her husband, what is mourning but just plain feeling sorry for *one's self*? There are long philosophical arguments leading up to that last statement, Doctor, but you're too busy to hear them right now. I'll give them to you later." He laughed, and walked on.

▶ 9. *Meet Your Problems with Decision*

In the multitude of practical problems you are obliged to meet in the course of living, you cannot possibly always be right, or make precisely the move that would be to your greatest advantage. But if, by and large, you can act using the principles and aids you are reading about in this chapter, your mistakes will not loom large or be very important.

Furthermore, *it is better to adjust your thinking to allowing and admitting a few mistakes than it is to keep milling and turning every little problem over and over in your mind.* Doing that results in a troubled, apprehensive outlook that will certainly produce E. I. I.

Of the total number of decisions we have to make, only a very small percentage will be improved as the result of long continued study and consideration. Also, a great many of the decisions fall into the same category as deciding whether one wants to buy the pink-flowered set of dishes, or the dishes with the gold design. These are decisions in which the issue is usually of a minor nature; either of two actions will do perfectly well.

The best rule to follow, therefore, is to make your decisions without a long huffing, puffing rumpus and fuss. Decide what you are going to do about a problem, then quit thinking about it.

One of my patients had a severe recurrent fibrositis, so severe that she would be in bed with it at times for weeks. No type of therapy would do the least bit of good. She was a very vigorous and self-assured individual, and I knew she would resent my telling her that her fibrositis was due to a wrong set of emotions. However, seeing her in a few of these attacks, I was certain that there was a recurring factor in her life that was responsible for her attacks.

I was planning on how I could most diplomatically bring this to her attention, when (to my relief), she offered her diagnosis of her own accord. "I think I know what is bringing these attacks on, Doctor. You may disagree with me, but I am sure by this time that there is some sort of a connection. My idea may be all wrong, but I've noticed that every time my husband gets into one of his terrible scrapes, I get an attack of my pain and have to go to bed."

"You are perfectly right," I assured her, "I was just getting ready to suggest the same thing."

"Well, Doctor," the poor woman asked, "How am I possibly going to handle it?"

"You must, of course, continue doing your best to help your husband, and get the best help for him. On the other hand, he has gotten himself into a particular rut which he is likely to stay in for some time. Every time he precipitates himself into a mess, and you know he will continue to do so, *decide at that time what you are going to do about it, then make yourself quit thinking about it*. It is turning the thing uselessly over and over in your mind, even after you know what course you will take, that is the thing that brings on your fibrositis."

She practiced this simple instruction with understandable difficulty at first. But it gradually became easier as she practiced, and the husband gave her plenty of practice. Finally, when the tremendous decisions came, which she always had feared would eventually come, she was well enough practiced that she could pass through them with a minimal amount of somatic disturbance, and had nothing nearly as severe as her old fibrositis.

Some decisions just can't be made. In our living we are apt to come upon a piece of trouble (and it is usually a tough, large piece) to which there is no apparent solution. The important thing in handling this variety of trouble is to tell ourselves that *there is no solution other than to* QUIT THINKING ABOUT THEM.

Mrs. K—— had a family of three children and a husband who had been drunk just about every day for fifteen years. The depths of misery to which that woman and that family descended are beyond simple description. Every possible treatment and approach had been tried to break the man of his drinking habit. None had more than a very short beneficial effect. For certain reasons, the woman did not wish to divorce him. Her misery, and the children's misery, grew deeper and deeper.

Then one day she came to an important decision.

She said to herself, "We had better give up the idea that Albert ever can, or ever will, stop drinking. From here on in, I'm not going to torture my mind anymore over Albert or his drinking. We'll take care of him, of course, but we'll quit worrying about him. Instead, I am going to devote every energy I have toward making the rest of my life, and my children's lives, as happy as they can possibly be under the circumstances."

She realigned herself in relation to her problem.

She was admitting that her problem was insoluble, and that there was no use expending any further worry or thinking upon it.

Her realigned efforts worked wonders. She was like a new woman. The children began to take on a new dignity in place of the beaten looks they had worn so long.

➡ 10. *Make the Present Moment an Emotional Success*

Getting rid of lousy emotional habits should not and need not be a complicated procedure. Above all, keep it simple. Reduce it to the terms of a common denominator — *keep your attitude and thinking as cheerful and pleasant as possible* — RIGHT NOW.

The only moment we ever live is the present moment. It is the only time *we ever have* to be happy.

Some people live on an expectancy basis, always looking for something in the future, completely losing the only value they have — that which is in the present moment.

The boy in high school anticipates college; in college, he anticipates the joy that will be his when he gets an engineering job. When he gets his engineering job, he believes that joy will come when he marries Mary and has a home; and so he goes on . . . anticipating.

There finally comes a time in his life when further anticipation is no longer rosy. That point is accompanied by a tremendous reorientation of thinking, values, and emotions. That is the point where the individual begins, visibly, to look old, licked, and beaten. At that point, too, anticipation is metamorphosed into thinking about the wonders and glories of the past (which are past).

Plan for the future, but don't brood on it. Naturally, we have to plan for the future, but we shouldn't make our present moment a constant thinking about it. Beyond the necessity of providentially planning the future, constant thinking of it and living in it entail fear, concern, and apprehension.

It is utterly silly to be constantly worrying about what the future may do to our affairs, cattle, health, children, yes, even our life after death. Being upset over the future isn't going to alter it a great deal. Most of our worries are interest we pay ahead of time on things that never happen.

The best insurance for a satisfactory future is to handle the present hour properly, do a good job of living now, be effective in your work, your thinking, your pleasantness, your helpfulness to other people, RIGHT NOW. Yes, RIGHT NOW. The future will turn out to be as good as your present if you keep on handling THE PRESENT MOMENT correctly. That's an important trick.

➤ 11. *Always Be Planning Something*

A basic psychological need in every person is the need for new experiences. Without new experience, life sags down into a rut of interminable drudgery.

To have *the expectation of* a new experience coming up is always a lift to the present moment, and you should always be planning an experience. It may be only a day's outing, or a half day of something on a Sunday, or merely a new feather in your hat. Your planning needn't be anything elaborate, except on rare occasions. The important thing is that it be *new experiences you are looking forward to.*

The planning is just as beneficial in supplying the right kind of emotions as is the new experience itself. Barney Olds, whom I could just as well have used instead of William as an example of the King of Living in chapter 8, was a man who had met one catastrophe after another with superb equanimity, resignation, determination, courage, and cheerfulness. He finally had an illness that kept him in bed for three months; then a recurrence kept him in bed for a solid year. He never complained.

I said to him once, "Barney, don't you get tired of being in bed?"

Barney laughed heartily, "No. I have a good appetite; that's half of living. *And every day I have a good cigar;* that's the other half."

Barney enjoyed life more, confined to bed, than most people do on a holiday. He loved to plan trips to distant parts of the world, to Tibet, Manga Reva, to Tasmania, and so forth. He would write to travel agencies and steamship companies for information. He would get books and literature from the library about the place he was "going to." At the end of each "trip" he knew as much about the land of his destination as though he had actually been there. One travel agency was afraid it was missing Barney's business, and sent a representative to see him. After that, the travel agency helped Barney play his game by sending him copies of official tickets to the places he was "visiting." Barney enjoyed himself all the more.

➤ 12. *Don't Let Irritating Things Get Your Goat*

In almost every moment there are worries or irritations that would get under your skin IF YOU LET THEM. It is hard to conceive of a single irritation, at least in the usual run of things, that *ever needs* to get under one's skin.

Whenever you are confronted with an irritation that is knocking and trying to get in, try the trick of forming the "magic circle" with your forefinger and thumb, holding it out before you, and say, "Nuts to that. I'm not going to let it get under my skin." A little practice with this magic circle and you will soon be able to say "Nuts" very agreeably and pleasantly to most of the potential irritations that come along.

➤ *The Best Part of Being Human Is That You Can Learn*

By including these twelve items in your general attitude, you will make a big stride toward emotional stasis and maturity. Living will begin to take on a general glow of enjoyability. You'll find yourself changing in very fundamental and effective ways; you'll begin to feel the grand feeling of "Boy, I feel good!" and life will become enjoyable.

The really best quality of human beings is that they can always learn something new, once they see the necessity for learning it. In my practice, I have seen hundreds of people rise to that capacity and turn themselves from a state of emotional stress to a creditable state of emotional stasis. If that hope and that possibility did not exist, I would long ago have left the practice of medicine for other fields, because more than half of the practice of medicine is curing E. I. I.

Before leaving this chapter, I wish to anticipate a question that is frequently brought up, "Why don't you include religion as one of your aids?"

➤ *Religion and Emotionally Induced Illness*

The answer is in no way a disparagement of religion.

It is true that many people are relieved of emotional stress when religious faith comes into their lives to occupy the vacuum that was made by the lack of one of the basic psychologic needs that are discussed in Chapter 14. These are people in whom there is a deep sense of insecurity, or people in whose lives there has been a great lack of affection or a minimum of recognition, or people who have a deep feeling of complete personal incompetence.

But it is equally true that religion, per se, neither increases nor decreases the individual's chances of getting E. I. I.

The clergy and strongly religious people have E. I. I. just as often as non-religious people.

One excellent minister, for instance, developed a very bothersome colon because of the terrific pressure of work that the great charge under his care entailed. Another good churchman had marked dizziness, weakness, and headache as a result of a prolonged and tough campaign to raise money for a new church. These, of course, are stresses of the type anyone might have. But sometimes the stress arises out of religion itself as in the case of the militant and crusading minister who was greatly concerned and disturbed over the wickedness of his small town congregation and who succeeded, after a violent campaign, in bringing them to do as he wished. The physical effect was a prolonged dyspepsia, which finally became a frank ulcer.

It is evident in medical practice that a religious person needs the attitudes we are presenting in this book just as much as the non-religious. As a matter of fact, the attitudes presented in this book will beautifully augment and complete religious living, because the attitudes that comprise maturity are exactly the things the great teachers of ethics have always been driving at.

KEY POINTS IN CHAPTER 9

Important Points to Watch in Living

* 1. Keep life simple.
* 2. Avoid watching for a knock in your motor.
* 3. Learn to like work.
* 4. Have a good hobby.
* 5. Learn to be satisfied.
* 6. Like people.
* 7. Say the cheerful, pleasant thing.
* 8. Turn the defeat of adversity into victory.
* 9. Meet your problems with decision.
* 10. Make the present moment a success.
* 11. Always be planning something.
* 12. Say "Nuts" to irritations.

10.   ACHIEVING EMOTIONAL STASIS IN THE FAMILY

➡ *The Family Is Our Number-One Cause of Disease*

The most important single educational factor to which most people are subjected is the family in which they grow up. Because of the amount of time a person spends in the family and the authoritative nature of the control which the family has over our early thinking the family has more to do with molding our personalities and our ability to handle living than any other factor.

In view of this tremendous effect the family has upon its charges, it is very sad that such a tremendous number of families are muffing their opportunities, and are doing a poor job.

It is very obvious, in seeing patients in the office, that our families are by far the greatest cause of wrong emotions our society has. Not only in their childhood families do so many people contract emotional stress, but equally in the families of which they have themselves become a head. The family –

our past family, and our present family — is by far the most common cause of E. I. I., by far our most prevalent disease.

The saddest part of this family failure is that with a small amount of steering the families that have been off-center for generations might be guided into the proper channel, where they would become an effective educational factor for good. But, as in other fields of emotional guidance, there are no organized programs for accomplishing such an improvement.

First, let us review the family atmospheres that produce immaturity and emotional stress.

➤ *Family Atmospheres That Produce Stress*

1. **A kill-joy atmosphere in the family.** One of the common family atmospheres productive of the wrong kind of emotions is the KILL-JOY ATMOSPHERE. In such families a dismal, pessimistic attitude toward everything prevails. "Oh, what do we want a picnic for anyway? It will probably rain; if it doesn't, the ants will eat everything up." In families like this, joy is nipped in the bud before it ever starts to bloom.

Betty came from a family like this, a family of constant gloom. Like the rest of her family, Betty had no sparkle or lustre; nor did any of her known ancestors. Her family life provided her with none of the qualities that would make her popular at school. Betty was passed over by the students and by the teachers; it wasn't a dislike they had for her, but she was so negative that she always faded out of consideration. She was just never invited to other children's homes because a gloomy atmosphere always attended her presence. Betty's mother never invited other children over to play with Betty because her mother was gloomy and didn't like fun. And, of course, Betty developed a gloomy attitude toward her own physiology, the same attitude her mother had regarding her own health.

By the time Betty was 13, she was a confirmed hypochondriac. She was apprehensive of every manifestation that her gloomy emotions produced, until her health, or her supposed lack of it, became her major concern. She joined the great and numerous Symptom-a-Day Club. When she awakened in the morning, her first thought would be, "How am I sick today?" After she was 13, Betty was not without medical attention any year of her life. Her apprehension concerning her health was strongly augmented by her mother's insistent concern. By the time she was 40, she had had four operations and a surgical menopause.

Betty's father, as well as her mother, was a glum pessimist, entirely taciturn and humorless. He was that way because of the family *he* was brought up in. The line of such families probably went back to neolithic times. He was the Sam, King of His Own Stew you read about in chapter 8 whose wife said that possibly he had said something pleasant the first year they were married, but that it was so long ago she could no longer be sure.

2. The critical atmosphere in the family. Another family atmosphere that breeds the wrong kind of emotions is the CRITICAL ATMOSPHERE. In such families, the atmosphere is charged with criticism of everybody. Usually the father starts it originally, but it becomes so universally prevalent among all the members of the family that all a visitor can say is, "Who flang that last brick?" An argument in the family is frequently this, "I'm not either losing my temper. You're the one who is losing your temper." As a matter of fact, all of them have permanently lost their tempers.

Barbara had the misfortune to have been born into a family like that. As she grew up she became, of course, the mirror of the family, and carried the atmosphere of criticism to school with her. In school she had a great deal of trouble because of her critical attitude toward the teacher and children. And at home her life consisted in running a critical gauntlet in which all the other members of the family were arraigned against her. At ten, Barbara had emotionally induced illness.

Cold war in the home. There are some families in which the critical atmosphere is maintained in the form of cold warfare instead of more or less open flinging of bricks. The criticism here is in the nature of sharp, cutting insinuations, often delivered in dulcet tones. Clifford was a master at this sort of thing; when he and his wife Betty had guests in of an evening, Clifford would get in a cutting criticism of Betty by saying at the bridge table, "Better not let Betty keep score, she'll just get our accounts hopelessly balled up," insinuating that Betty couldn't keep her household accounts straight. Or he might say conversationally, "At our house we never know when or where we're going to eat until the can is opened."

This sort of thing, which went on year after year, always hurt Betty a great deal, and as time went on, Betty was sick a great part of the time with emotionally induced illness. Notice that Clifford, who was responsible, was hit by the boomerang of having to pay the medical bills.

Critical influences from outside the family. Sometimes an illness-producing stream of criticism may issue from an odd source in an otherwise normal family. Jane was a fine girl and married George, a fine boy, who was deeply in love with her, and who, in a very understanding way, took good care of Jane. Jane's life was going along splendidly until she brought her first-born home from the hospital. George secured the services of a practical nurse to help Jane with the housework and with the baby.

This practical nurse was an old-timer who knew everything better than Jane did, or the doctor did, for that matter, and she openly criticized the way in which Jane was handling the baby. She would criticize everything, including the formula the pediatrician had given the baby. She would make remarks, "I don't think the baby is getting along well. There is something wrong with it; it just doesn't act like a baby should." Then Jane would cart the baby off to the pediatrician who would assure Jane that the baby was perfectly all right. Whereupon, back home, Old Battle-ax would remark, "Well, you know sometimes these doctors don't tell you everything."

As this sort of thing continued, Jane began to feel poorly

without knowing why. George and the doctor, at first, did not know what was wrong, either. Then they both caught on. Jane was a capable girl, intelligent and alert. Her baby was a great event to her, a great challenge and opportunity for intelligent, creative motherhood. But the Old Battle-ax had completely deflated Jane's confidence in herself and had sent her into a state of constant worry and deep-seated concern. When the doctor and George found Jane's trouble, the remedy was simple and George applied it promptly. He fired the Old Battle-ax. Jane was soon getting along fine.

The remedy isn't always that simple. Barbara, for instance, couldn't fire her father and mother.

3. The atmosphere of dislike. Another common family atmosphere which produces the wrong kind of emotions is the ATMOSPHERE OF DISLIKE, or the atmosphere of lack of affection, an atmosphere that is fatal to anything good that the family as an institution stands for.

Usually this atmosphere of dislike stems from the basic fact that father and mother do not like each other, and the only reason they hang together is "for the children's sake." In the atmosphere of such a home, the children quickly learn not to like each other. Love, or dislike, comes to children largely by example. The parents have no genuine affection for the children, and the children reciprocate with even less.

In this kind of family nobody wants any of the other members. No one is necessary to anyone else, and when a person feels he isn't necessary, he never develops full mature individuality. No one in a family like this is made to feel important or desirable for himself. No one ever gives or receives any appreciation. Life is like eating dried, tasteless prunes.

Ellen was the youngest of seven children in a home where no one really cared about anyone else. Being the youngest, she was the target of everyone else's ill will. Every member of the family was criticizing Ellen as soon as she was old enough to understand. "Oh, she's dumb." "She isn't going to be able to get through school." No one ever helped Ellen. By the time she got into school, she had a deeply grounded inferiority complex. She looked past her teachers because everyone told her she was stupid. When Ellen, after a hectic childhood, at last grew up, she married a boy who had had the same kind of a past and the same kind of an inferiority complex. When she had children, she was sure she lacked the ability to rear them; she had no confidence in her ability as a housewife. Hers was a constant life of worry.

Ellen has been sick most of the time since childhood and is still sick today. It is not so easy to correct the factors in her illness as it was in the case of Jane, George, and the Old Battle-ax.

4. The atmosphere of selfish egoism. Another family atmosphere that breeds the wrong kind of emotions is the ATMOSPHERE OF SELFISH EGOISM, which is a little different from the atmosphere of criticism, although it, too, usually starts with the father.

Virginia, who had been doing all right alone, married a boy who was a pathological egoist of the kind whose only concern is himself. This was not immediately apparent in Roger because he was the kind of an egoist who doesn't talk about himself. But every thought he had was for himself. When Virginia married him, of course, she didn't know what she was getting into.

Roger was decent enough, but he used Virginia solely for his own purposes. Roger was addicted to hunting and fishing; and that's what he was forever doing — without taking Virginia along. Outside of that, he liked to play cards, and bowl; so he did that. Virginia was alone at home most of the time. Roger liked only a few foods, so they were what the family ate. Roger's work took him on the road much of the time, and Virginia was alone at home bringing up one, two, three, and four children. When Virginia began to complain about not feeling well, Roger had no sympathy and no patience.

Today, Virginia is a very sick girl and her health will not readily be brought back to normal. Roger does not see what *he* has to do with her health, and he now regards Virginia as an obstruction to his pleasure. Virginia's children are maladjusted and are functionally ill too.

5. **The complaining atmosphere.** Another bad atmosphere in a family is the COMPLAINING ATMOSPHERE. No family is more miserable than the one that has in it a perennial and perpetual bellyacher. Most often the bellyacher is the mother, although I have seen families in which it is the father.

When a family contains someone who is constantly complaining, there is no possible enjoyment for anyone. These complainers awaken in the morning and start analyzing themselves for symptoms. It's usually easy to find a symptom somewhere, especially in the morning before you've had breakfast Every one of us has a pain somewhere or other most of the time, if we wish to make something of it. If you ask yourself, as you sit there, "Where do I hurt?" you can find a place that hurts. These complainers are forever looking for those places and allowing their minds to play over the painful areas all day long. The most pitiful part is that they paddle the rest of the family with their miseries.

In 99 cases out of 100, these complainers have nothing more wrong with them than an emotionally induced illness, but to hear them expound on their health, you would think they were fully equipped pathological museums. In the family they succeed in producing an atmosphere of gloom and anxiety, and these are the elements the children acquire. Gloom, anxiety, and hypochondriasis is the educational influence such families give their children.

In addition to making the family miserable, these complainers are poison to the bank account. One lady had, during the course of her miserable life, seen fifteen doctors, four cultists, two spiritualists, and had eight operations, had been in three sanitaria, and had spent a total of $32,000.

6. **The atmosphere of fear and anxiety in the family.** One businessman I know gets up in the morning with an anxiety, and jumps anxiously from one anxiety to the next until he goes to bed, and then keeps himself awake with more anxieties.

For instance, *every morning* he hesitates and debates what particular tie he will wear, and sometimes goes into a dither over it. At breakfast he worries whether he is using too much sugar on his cereal and immediately wonders whether he has diabetes. Driving downtown to work he will debate with himself whether to take one street or another and, having taken one, worries that he should have taken the other, lest fate decree that he have an accident on the street he is on. Coming to his store he worries about the show windows and about the whistling of one of his clerks.

His family has caught the same worrying habit — it's very contagious. His wife picked it up; his children have grown up in it. To them, it is the normal, natural way to live. They just haven't experienced any other way.

Some day, if they are lucky, they may be released from the habit sufficiently to realize they are unhappy, that they are personally maladjusted, and that they have emotionally induced illness.

7. **The atmosphere of in-law domination.** Another atmosphere that can be very bad for the family's emotions is the ATMOSPHERE OF IN-LAW DOMINATION. In-law domination may be very obvious and yet not easy to deal with.

Helen was a fine young lady who hailed from Philadelphia. She married a young man and went to live in his home town, a small village of 250, loaded with his relatives, some of whom were banshees. Some of these relatives saw Helen settled in a new, modern house and felt that Helen was getting the deal *they* deserved but didn't get. They made good every opportunity to pick on Helen, to hurt her in little underhanded ways. Helen became ill, and after a while she was too sick to work. Then the banshee relatives really swooped down on her like vultures, and finished her up. After that, the only time Helen ever felt well was when she returned to Philadelphia for a month's visit. In the course of a few years she became practically incapacitated by functional disease. She was finally carried off the battlefield by the divorce court, and within a year she was back to her normal self. Ever since then she has been well.

Young people should live by themselves. With few exceptions, it is best for young people, just starting out, to live independently and far enough removed from their elders to have complete control and command of their own families. In close proximity, parents are always finding it easy to offer suggestions, if not orders, a thing which neighbors do only when asked, but a thing which parents are apt to do when not asked. In one family where the newlyweds lived in the same house with the parents, the mother-in-law was well-meaning and only wished to be helpful. The daughter-in-law, too, wished, above all, to get along with the mother-in-law. They did get along, seemingly very nicely, but with the mother in the lead and guiding position, which frustrated the daughter-in-law's need for independent, creative living. In-laws, grandmothers, and grandfathers had best live apart from the children and allow the children an independent life.

➡ *A Family Doesn't Need to Be a Bad Influence*

Those we have reviewed are, of course, only a few of the bad atmospheres that make our families our most important breeding ground for disease. In a physician's office, it becomes apparent that a great many families are doing a perfectly rotten job and are providing their members with the wrong kind of emotions. Many other families are not doing as good a job as they might.

The pitfalls that a family can fall into are so numerous that it might seem discouraging to the well-intentioned home-maker or the intelligent newlywed.

However, there is no need for discouragement.

If you introduce into the family atmosphere the same rules that bring emotional stasis to the individual, you will have a family whose influence on its members is a healthy one. You will have an atmosphere which develops maturity. You will have a family that is a unit of enjoyable life for everyone in it.

➡ *Home Is the Place Where —*

Robert Frost once said, "Home is the place where, when you have to go there, they have to let you in."

We can paraphrase that to define what a home *should be*: "A good home is the place where, when you desperately need a lift, you'll be sure to find one." *A lift,* you understand, not more irritation, not nagging, not arguments, not a scathing look, not a lack of sympathy, but a LIFT.

Your first job, as a member of your family, is to keep your attitude and your thinking calm and cheerful — RIGHT NOW.

Your second job is to help the other members of your family keep their attitudes and thinking calm and cheerful RIGHT NOW.

Here are a few ingredients to work into the daily living of your family:

➡ *Family Atmospheres That Produce Emotional Stasis and Maturity*

1. **Emphasize simplicity in living and simplicity in enjoyment.** As the American standard of living has increased, a greater and greater array of mechanisms have been dangled invitingly before the consumers' eyes. The trend in American living has been to put so much emphasis on the means for enjoyment — fine houses, automobiles, better television sets, cameras, electric ranges — that in the process of getting the means, we provide ourselves with frustration and anxieties. Yearning, longing, and then paying the installments become so constant we never learn how, indeed, we never have the opportunity to learn how, just simply to *enjoy.*

The way to proceed is to learn the art of enjoyment first. Minimize the need, or the longing in the family, for new installments. RIGHT NOW enjoy what there *is*: the green of the trees, the blue of the skies, your own whistling, having fun with each other. Leave out conversation of yearning for what you haven't.

The idea is to utilize the little, ever-present opportunities for pleasantry, the immediately available chances for a humorous sally, the RIGHT NOW moment for being nice to each other.

2. **Get the idea of the family enterprise.** As soon as the children are old enough to understand, indoctrinate them with the idea that the family is meant to be a wonderful place for everybody in it; it's everybody's job to make it a wonderful place for everybody else; it's an enterprise for everybody, by *everybody*. The family enterprise is a cooperative effort in which father, mother, sister, brother, all have an active interest and a personal responsibility. The family enterprise is the primary and most important activity and responsibility that father, mother, brother and sister have.

Don't forget this; the children will acquire and carry on the family enterprise if mother and *father* do their share. Usually it's the father who is just a boarding and bored member, always off to business, the races, and Heaven knows where. If the top brass takes the proper initiative, the children will invariably follow.

The family enterprise becomes a continual round of mutual projects, of things done together, games played together, stories told around the fire, group studies of interesting things and places, Sunday afternoon nature jaunts, yearly family trips to the fair, laughter, conversation, and gaiety *that everyone* (and that includes father) engages in and which everyone helps everyone else to enjoy.

3. **Attach the family to the human enterprise.** An important idea to get into family living is that the family is in tune with the wide community which surrounds it. Beside the responsibility the members have to one another in the family enterprise, they have a similar responsibility to the HUMAN ENTERPRISE. This is quite a necessary step in the development of the children's maturity. It is part of that aspect of maturity which consists in turning our ego away from purely selfish considerations out toward the welfare of others. Never to develop this sense of the human enterprise is to bury

ourselves for life in a pit of very stinky little emotions. If the children get the idea that the most important thing for anyone is the welfare and the happiness of the other people in our individual-community, they will have the instrument for producing a highly satisfactory emotional color, and they will find that life is filled with the highest kind of enjoyment.

Furthermore, the idea of the human enterprise in the family brings to the members of the family a kindliness, a sympathy, and an understanding for other people, *which you cannot live happily without.*

Part of the family enterprise consists in projects directed toward meeting, knowing, and helping the great wide world outside: parties, "get to know your neighbors" picnics, family trips through industrial plants, family trips into the great wide world, adopting a war orphan, other projects that the family can, as they go about them, specifically label "Human Enterprise." Getting to use the name "Family Enterprise" for one type of activity and the name "Human Enterprise" for another, in itself teaches maturity and awareness of purpose in the children. Whatever helps the children is sure to help father and mother.

4. Develop a family ability for turning defeat into victory. Whatever happens, when events occur that might disappoint or frustrate, the attitude in the family should always be, "We are not going to let that get us down; we are going to make the best of it, and the best is going to be pretty good!" This gets easier and easier to do, and as the family becomes competent in its use, there will be very little that can sour the family's day.

The particular maturity that is taught to the children by the tactic of turning defeat into victory is *flexibility and adaptability.*

The family is all set to go to Parfrey's Glen on a picnic when the rain begins to pour; so what? — yipee — it's just as much fun playing games in the living room with the picnic later on the living room floor.

Handling the lesser upsets in that way makes it easier to

meet the tougher assignments. Mother gets sick and goes to the hospital; everyone pitches in, not only on the work, but in holding up the family morale and mother's morale. It's doubly important, then, that every member keep the family clicking with heads up and chins out.

The trick of turning defeat into victory can become a game, with everyone trying to see who has the best solution for licking the upset, and then all cooperating on the best suggestion.

5. **Without affection, the family is a failure.** General affection is easily generated in a family if there is affection between father and mother. Affection must include everyone equally and must not be partial. Everyone is made to feel necessary and indispensable to the general family operations. Animosities between the children need never exist if they are nipped in the early bud, and if no animosities ever exist between father and mother. If there is bickering, strife, and verbal warfare in the top brass section of the family, the children will almost surely grow up to be bickering and disagreeable. They in turn get married and start another cycle of foolish disagreement and bickering.

A doctor gets tired of seeing these silly nincompoops who lose most of their affection for each other before the first year of marriage is over. It is so completely childish and unnecessary. The answer to any marriage is that you should be mature enough to rise above the problems it entails. With ten cents' worth of good intentions, a nickel's worth of sympathy, and a quarter's worth of understanding, affection would grow through the years.

If the parents have affection, one of the rules in the family can be that no one is *ever* to quarrel or bicker with anyone else. That rule is not hard to maintain if the example comes from the top.

6. **The general tone should be kindly cheerfulness.** There is no such thing as the "dumps" in families where everyone pitches in to help the one who, because of some outside factor, needs a lift. Such a home is the place where, when you need a lift, you'll find it.

Here again the example is set by the top brass. If the parents never get crabby at one another, or allow themselves the misery of feeling lousy and mean, a rule in the family can be that no one is to engage in this nefarious activity.

7. **Discipline should be reasonable, firm, yet pleasant.** Parents in unhappy families probably will not believe this, but in a happy family there isn't much call for discipline. Misbehaving children are unhappy children. If the children are provided with a happy, pleasant atmosphere, two-thirds of your disciplinary problems disappear.

Children must be taught certain fundamentals, like respect for others' rights and for others as individuals. They should be taught to respect their elders; they should be taught the advisability of not flouting convention and living well within the law. Honesty and integrity are absolute requisites.

There will be times, of course, when discipline will be necessary. Then discipline should be based on the reasonable ground that we act thus and so because that way of acting is for our own good, and we do not act otherwise because it is bad for us and bad for those around us. This basis for action can be explained just as well in a pleasant, well-meaning manner; it adds nothing to do it in a fit of splenic anger. For a wrong action there should be corrective explanation, and then a disciplinary measure carried forward without wavering or retracting. Punishment twice for the same offense will hardly ever be necessary.

8. **The family should instill confidence into its members.** It is important that the family should give the child a feeling of confidence — not only confidence in financial security, even if it isn't there, but confidence in his place in the family as someone who is respected for himself and as someone who has an important responsibility in contributing to the welfare and enjoyment of the family. No child, however awkward or backward he may be, must be made to feel that he is any less useful or important to the family.

Thus a basic psychological need is satisfied and a step in the development of an important aspect of maturity is made.

9. Mutual enjoyment in the family — right now. An indispensable idea in the family is that family living is a series of mutual enjoyments — every moment and RIGHT NOW. It *means* mutual enjoyment to its members, a pleasant quip or a jolly phrase when father passes son in the hall, or when Mary comes into the kitchen with mother. The family means mutual enjoyment, the glad word, the bit of fun, the happy smile — RIGHT NOW.

RIGHT NOW, of course; "What are we waiting for — why wait — this is the time — right now — right now is the time to show affection — now is the time to operate the Family Enterprise — *this* is the moment — why wait any longer?" It is perfectly all right to plan for the future, but don't spend your present in the future.

➤ *How Does Your Family Rate?*

Stop right now and ask yourself, "What kind of a family do I belong to?" Is it the kind of an enterprise that is producing the wrong kind of emotions, functional disease, personal maladjustments, and unhappiness? If it is, be fair to yourself and admit it.

Then take the next step: Set an example.

And the next step: Hold a get-together with your wife or your husband, include the children if they are old enough, and talk this over, lay plans to have the kind of a family where, when your spirits are low, you will be sure to find a lift.

THE IMPORTANT POINTS TO REMEMBER IN CHAPTER 10

Your family will become a center of good, happy living, and an influence for maturity and emotional stasis in its members, if you introduce into the family these things:

- 1. Simplicity in living, and simplicity in enjoyment.
- 2. The idea of the family enterprise.
- 3. The idea that the family is part of the human enterprise.
- 4. A family attitude for turning defeat into victory.
- 5. An atmosphere of affection, mutual respect, and regard.
- 6. A general tone of kindly cheerfulness.
- 7. Reasonable, firm, yet pleasant discipline.
- 8. A feeling of mutual confidence and security.
- 9. An atmosphere of enjoyment — RIGHT NOW.

11.

**HOW TO ATTAIN
SEXUAL MATURITY**

There is one *very* important spot in human living in which people's education has been either *nothing at all* or *worse* than nothing at all. That spot, of course, is sex.

More people show immaturity in their sexual life than in any other field of human activity. That is why doctors see so many people whose emotional stress is intimately related to immaturity in sex and sexual matters. There are a tremendous number of people who have made a mess of sex, or sex has made a mess of them.

Maturity in any field has to be learned. How can you possibly blame anyone for an immaturity in sex when no sensible effort is made to show him how to become mature? Where but on society and its institutions responsible for education — the family, the school, the church — does the blame rest for sexual delinquency, sexual stress, sexual mess?

➧ *Biology and Civilization*

The sex instinct is a relatively weak instinct compared to

some of the others. The biological urge for food is *much* stronger, and so is the desire for security. A person can go for a long time, even for a lifetime, without satisfying the sex urge, but no one can stand food and security deprivation very long.

The relative insignificance of the sex instinct is further apparent in the fact that the cooperative effort we call "civilization" is mainly an attempt to supply food and security, *not sexual satisfaction*. Had the sex instinct been the strongest and most demanding of our biological urges, civilization would, doubtless, have been patterned to supply sexual satisfaction.

The biological urges being what they are, and civilization being the kind of thing it is, everyone can be allowed to be promiscuous in eating, or promiscuous in developing security, but it became apparent thousands of years ago that the very basis of civilized society would be destroyed if everyone were to be allowed to be promiscuous sexually. The social and economic consequences of complete sexual promiscuity would be simply catastrophic.

The restraints are necessary. Granting that we want the economic benefits of a cooperative enterprise like civilization, we have taken the only course in regard to the sexual instinct that we possibly could have taken. That course has been to put the sexual instinct into well defined shackles of restraint. And *that* is what provides our sex problem.

The only way to shackle a thing as fundamental as a biological instinct, without upsetting the individual, is to develop a good educational process for showing the individual how he can possibly manage the instinct within its shackles. *But civilization had to curb the instinct long before it developed wisdom enough to devise an educational process.*

Is it any wonder we have the trouble with sex we do? You've got to be careful how you put a cork in a bottle of highly charged liquid. Either the cork will blow out or the bottle will burst.

The more you study a tough problem like sex, the more you become amazed that we human beings get along as well as we do, and the more you become convinced that the bunch of us are pretty remarkable little people. The whole race muddles through.

➡ *The Sex Urge Is Not the Mainspring of the Human Being*

Sigmund Freud and the psychoanalysts have developed the idea that sex is the mainspring of the human personality. It is true that sex causes a great deal of trouble for people for the reasons set forth above, but not because it is the mainspring. It isn't. Sex is, as human biological urges go, a relatively little spring that has been jumping all over the box. It is a spring that has been jumping all over the box because of these factors:

1. Every person is equipped with the sex urge.

2. The structure of our civilization makes it imperative to curb this urge to a very considerable extent, so that it still serves the purpose of reproducing our kind without upsetting social and economic structures.

3. Although society makes such a curb necessary, society makes no organized effort to show people how they can handle their urge without trouble to themselves.

4. There are numerous agencies, within society, deliberately fanning up people's sexual desires, largely because they find it profitable to do so.

Many commercial enterprises capitalize on shaking up the fizz in the charged bottle. These efforts to shake up the fizz have never been as prevalent as they have been in the last fifty years, and are one of the chief reasons why one out of three marriages is ending in divorce.

Commercial advertising, newspapers, magazines, movies, television, find "cheesecake" attractive to the unrequited yearnings and earnings of a sexually-uneducated public. It helps roll the dollars in, but is hard on those whose excited sexual desires get them into emotional or legal trouble.

Some youth (or immature adult) who is having trouble trying to adjust his sexual inclinations opens a magazine (any of our better weekly magazines) and he finds stimulating "cheesecake" on every other page. The sexual longings that he has been trying to stifle are freshly stimulated, his imagination is stimulated, and a fresh set of stressing emotions are stimulated. If he stops there, the youth (or the immature adult) is just plain lucky. He may go on to get into trouble.

➡ The Popular Brand of So-Called Sophistication Is Immature

"Sophistication" has become a popular concept in the mid-20th-century United States. A person is not in the mode if he is not "sophisticated," by which is meant a varying degree of looseness concerning sexual taboos. There are, of course, various levels, or depths, of sophistication, beginning with sexy stories in open mixed society (the more shriekingly daring, obviously the more sophisticated) and progressing in ten easy lessons to situations of grossly illegal intimacy, in which the intimacy gradually becomes rancid and the illegality ever more bitter.

The philosophy underlying sophistication assumes that sophistication *is* sexual maturity — maturity in the same sense we defined it in chapter 7, namely, that *maturity is the capacity to handle human living with a minimum of trouble and a maximum of enjoyment.*

There are two distinct parts to the philosophy of sophistication. Some people subscribe only to the first part; others go along with both parts.

The first part states that treating sex as an unmentionable human misfortune, to be regarded definitely as a sordid affair to be admitted reluctantly even into marriage, is merely to increase the amount of misery that the tromped-upon sex urge can produce. This first part of the philosophy of sophistication is, doubtless, correct. I am in full accord with it.

The second part of the philosophy of sophistication is that sex constitutes a major sport that is always in season, that licenses are free, and the game is to be pursued through all the byways of so-called romance.

This second part is a gross error, as most of those discover who have to learn the hard way. Almost without exception, the apple that is picked turns out to be much less of a pippin than it seemed to be on the tree; and worse still, it contains a large worm of discomfiture. The miscreant realizes too late that it is much easier to stay out of trouble than to get out of it once he is in it.

➡ The Trouble with So-Called Sophistication

A person who has strong sexual urges that he represses and denies can develop a severe and serious, acute and chronic, anxiety state. But the person who resorts to the liberation of "sophistication" will suffer equally severe anxiety states. He can bring himself, as I shall show you in a moment, to the brink of considering and committing suicide. There is no anxiety state more advanced than that.

Even short of the state in which suicide becomes a consideration, the devotee of "sophistication" has other anxiety backgrounds. Being apprehended by the law, or being dragged before a court is neither the major trouble nor its culmination. There is the personal degrading effect of lying, the constant fear of apprehension, the feeling of guilt. Then there is the broken home; or worse, a home in which things are not going smoothly; or still worse, a home in which growing children are being brought up in a poor atmosphere.

What a silly, foolish, "sophisticated" adult does to himself is to a considerable extent his business. But it leaves the realm of private affairs when children are ruined for life because their family gave them wrong emotional patterns and habits.

Even the sophisticate acknowledges the futility of "sophistication" when he has arrived at the point where he is ready to jump from a bridge or reach for a pistol. No system of action is mature or good that can possibly bring a person to the brink of suicide. And "sophistication" can. Let me give you a couple of examples.

➡ Anything That Can Lead to Suicide Is Best Omitted

Richard Roe was a smart, quiet fellow. At least *he* thought he was. He meant no harm to anyone. He was a good husband, and a good father. Also, he didn't intend to be exactly mid-Victorian. Well, you know — it wasn't infatuation for another woman — not that kind of "triangle" thing, just an arrangement with a person of the other sex who, too, wasn't exactly mid-Victorian, but, shall we say, merely modern or advanced.

Richard carried on for a long time without anyone being the wiser (not even Richard). He thought, "This isn't hurting anyone else. I wouldn't want it to." He met the girl in various ways, at various places.

Then one night they were at a motel they had often frequented. The manager suspected an irregularity and intercepted the couple in the midst of a tryst. Richard had registered under an assumed name as husband of the lady. He was in a legal "spot." In fact, he was in a hot spot. He and the lady left before the police could be called, but the manager had secured his right name and address.

For two days Richard sweated. He came to see me because of indigestion — and told me his trouble. In addition to a physician, he had gone to a lawyer, too.

Believe me, *there was a miserable man*. He was trying to stave off utter and complete disaster. Mind you — UTTER AND COMPLETE DISASTER. For two days, Richard was as miserable as any human being could be. Physically *he felt terrible*, and he needed medical aid.

On the third day the hotel manager filed his complaint;

at ten-thirty, Richard was given the summons; at ten-forty-five Richard had put a bullet through his head.

The newspapers did not print news of the summons. They printed news of Richard's death. The reason why Richard died never got out. The family honor was saved. Richard was not. Richard was dead.

Doctor Mac, let us call him, was a nice sort of a guy, until he decided to give in to the urge and look at life in a broad, serene way. (Without any malice, you understand, but why shouldn't there be a little fun? After all, there are the Kinsey reports.)

So he made advances and the affair went on, until his accomplice became pregnant. Seeing the commercial value of her situation, she refused to let the doctor perform an illegal abortion (she would have had him there, too) but threatened him with suit.

The woman had come to me for examination when she thought she was pregnant, and told me the story in a boastful sort of way. Doctor Mac faced complete ruin — the suit would have thrown things wide open, of course. But more than that, in the state in which Mac lived, immoral conduct would cost him his medical license to practice. Knowing that the woman was just as responsible for the affair as was the doctor, I tried to talk her out of her intended law suit. She was too silly to listen.

On the first inkling that she had seen a lawyer to start a suit, Doctor Mac committed suicide by taking arsenic. Everyone thought he died a natural death. I never saw the woman anymore, but I read of her drowning a month later.

➤ More Often, the Trouble with Sophistication Lies This Side of Suicide

Alwin had been a pretty stable fellow and an astute businessman. Then he came to my office with something obviously functional. He tried to act his usual self. He swore he had nothing to upset him or worry him. His trouble became more acute and gradually took a new course. He was apprehensive and worried, which was unusual for him. I told him he wasn't fooling anyone by playing anxious-free, and jokingly suggested he was having an affair. Whereupon, he unfolded a lurid tale. He hadn't met any legal noose, like Richard or Mac had, but he was worried just the same.

➤ It Is Easier to Stay Out of Trouble Than to Get Out

The point in all this is, why start out on a track that can lead to a spot where suicide becomes a serious consideration, or. short of that, a course that can result in serious emotional illness?

There are communities in which sexual irregularity has become so accepted that discovery is not often attended by anything as drastic as suicide. But I know from personal conversations with the doctors in such areas that functional illness holds a terrifically large place in the lives of the people in these communities.

➤ Other Forms of Sexual Immaturity Besides "Sophistication"

I have talked about "sophistication" first because so many people mistakenly consider it to be sexual maturity. But there are other forms of sexual immaturity that produce much more emotional stress than does "sophistication."

A doctor's office during the course of a year sees many people with emotionally induced illness because they have brought sexual immaturity into marriage. Less often we see young people, or unmarried people, to whom sexual immaturity is also a source of emotional stress.

➤ Sexual Difficulties before Marriage

Youth is as innocent in the awakening of his sex curiosity as he was in his desire to eat, but the attitude of his elders makes the whole business seem at once bad and yet darkly inviting and mysterious. He is ordered to abstain, and then subjected to numerous varieties of sexual suggestion. Finally, the intimacy and privacy necessary for experimentation are only as far away as the car in the family garage. It, of course, isn't, and wasn't even in the horse and buggy days, anything like a good or a healthy set-up.

Then we add the final spice, which is that, owing to economic circumstances, marriage must be delayed ten or fifteen years beyond the awakening of the urge.

Here is a spot where a little planning by society, or the development of an educational method, would be an excellent thing. As it is, the advice these young people get is pretty poor and misleading stuff.

Youth's sexual urge leads them in one of three directions. First, the youth may be lucky enough to have someone with the necessary amount of good sense steer him, or her, in the less troublesome direction.

Secondly, they may break down the barriers and experiment with sex; possibly they may break down the barriers forcibly and come up for assault or murder. If they cross the barriers amiably, they precipitate themselves into the types of trouble we spoke of above. Thirdly, they may take masturbation as a way out.

➡ Masturbation Is Often the Source of Poor Emotions

Many people come to the doctor with emotionally induced illness because they are worried and apprehensive over a strong, unconquerable habit of masturbating.

For instance, a twenty-eight-year-old single woman had tiredness, headaches, and a long string of symptoms because she was sure that her habit of masturbating was wrecking the foundations of her health. Her symptoms had become more severe after she found and read an old family health guide in which the writer stated that masturbation is invariably followed by such dire physical consequences as sterility, tumors, heart disease, cancer, and insanity. The author of that article was a far more enthusiastic moralizer than scientist, a fact which the poor lady did not know. She felt that she had all the physical degeneration described by the author, and she was certain that her mind was going too. She had arrived at the point where she was unable to do her usual work.

There is another variety of poor emotions that results from masturbating, that is even more prone to produce E. I. I These emotions arise because masturbating causes the indi vidual to withdraw into himself and into a dream world of his own making. He develops introvert tendencies, lives in social isolation, and prefers to live in his world of dreams and fantasies. As a consequence, he lacks effectiveness in the real world; he lacks decisiveness; he staggers along through life, unproductive, unhappy, and alone. His emotions are predominantly brooding, regretful, and generally unhappy. He or she presents a sad regressing picture.

To put it simply — masturbation *is* immaturity. It is a childish way of satisfying one of the basic needs. Just as with other forms of immaturity, it is bound to be unsuccessful in a world which calls for maturity.

➡ *Sexual Perversion As a Source of Poor Emotions*

There are, of course, people made miserable by the guilt, the difficulties, or the stigmata encountered by following one of the many types of sexual perversion, of which there are 14 or 15 different varieties, the most common being homosexuality. Sex perversions are evidence of deeply-seated personality difficulties that require individualized treatment.

Consequently, we will dismiss further discussion of the perversions in this book, except to offer assurances to the reader that boys and girls whose lives are rich with outside interests, who have had good training at home in thinking and acting carefully and critically, do not develop sexual perversions.

Nor need parents be afraid about the danger of their sons and daughters coming in contact with homoerotics and thus being misled into unnatural sexual relations. Careful investigations disclose that the individuals who take up homosexuality were definitely homosexuals before they met their seducer.

Another misconception that requires correction is that it is the man who is markedly feminine, or the woman who is markedly masculine, who is most apt to be homoerotic. There is not the slightest connection. The male homoerotic is just as apt to be the athletic masculine type, and the female homoerotic a perfect feminine type. The unfortunate feminine man and the unfortunate masculine woman have enough of a handicap without adding this misconception.

➡ *Sexual Immaturity in Marriage*

Sexual difficulties in marriage are extremely frequent, extremely provocative of emotional stress, extremely apt to start the schism that leads to divorce, and are always caused by sexual immaturity on the part of one or (usually) both the partners. There are many varieties, of course, of sexual difficulties in marriage, and we can mention only the most frequent here.

The difficulties start most often on the honeymoon, which to most newlyweds is the end of the dream world youth paints of the marital state. The *usual* experience on the honeymoon is that the boy and the girl find that it isn't as wonderful as they thought it would be, and they blame each other. If the boy and the girl can overlook the first years in which their experiences are vaguely somewhere between success and failure, they may find at the end of 30 years that the experience *can* be the rainbow they found it wasn't on their honeymoon.

Most young men, when first married, have the imagination of rabbits, the romantic capacity of sloths, and the sexual technique of oysters. When you mix this combination with the fears, the discomforts, and the misinformation which the girl has accumulated, you end up with nights filled with horrible experiences.

If a fair amount of maturity exists in the couple, such as sympathy, understanding, comradeship, and good-will, all may not yet be lost and the marital craft may yet be rescued before it founders. But with many couples, who have no maturity in other directions to save their sexual immaturity, the disillusionment of the beginning grows into the final break of the end.

When sexual immaturity brings one, or both, of the partners into the doctor's office with E. I. I., it is very apt to center around frigidity in the woman. Over 40 per cent of the married women I see in my practice get no sexual enjoyment out of their marriage, and provide little enjoyment for their husbands. Wife happy? No — miserable. Husband happy? No — just as miserable.

Frigidity is most often the husband's fault. Much of this frigidity on the part of the wife is not her fault, but is due primarily to the clumsy, selfish technique of the husband, not merely in the first delicate experiences of marriage, but forever after.

As many women put it, "He has not thought of anything but his own wishes. He leaves me cold and disgusted. Now it only makes me nervous. I hate the whole thing."

You will always find that these husbands are immature children in other aspects of living as well as in sex. Mentally, their maturity stopped at age eight; physically, they went on to develop hair on their chests. Many an otherwise excellent girl has been precipitated into chronic illness and chronic unhappiness by this common variety of inept and immature husband. Even though she may try to meet the situation philosophically, the situation proves to be too difficult.

Frigidity may be the result of faulty education. In a relatively smaller number of women, such frigidity is sometimes the result of poor sex education in their childhood. Rose, for instance, was the unusually attractive daughter of a family that lived in a tough part of town. Because of the bad influences of the neighborhood, the mother stringently indoctrinated the young Rose against the entire matter of sex, scaring her on the entire subject until Rose had the idea that sexual intercourse was far and away the worst experience that could ever befall a woman, that it was, in fact, worse than death. Rose never did know why or just how she ever became married. Marriage for her was a hateful, hideous experience. After bearing two children, conceived in utter agony, Rose added the fear of another pregnancy to her already unwholesome sex outlook. She developed an intractable ulcerative colitis and has spent years in and out of hospitals.

Frigidity in the wife is an important cause of yet another grave marital difficulty — unfaithfulness in the husband. As one English Earl remarked, he greatly preferred to have his romantic efforts returned by the appreciative and enthusiastic embraces of the chambermaid than to suffer the reluctant frigidity of the Countess. Every man, earl or no earl, is made of the same material.

Appetite is not the same in both partners. Another common source of difficulty in marriage is a failure on the part of the partners to recognize the *usual* difference in sexual appetites in man and woman. In general, men are moved by the sexual instinct more frequently than are women. Unless this difference is appreciated by the partners, and each tries to meet the difference at least half way, irritation, disgruntlement, and deep displeasure are bound to result. This common situation can be avoided only if each has enough maturity to appreciate the individual needs and desires of the other.

There are many other varieties of difficulties arising in the complex relations of marriage. We are not going to review them, but deal with them merely by saying that they all, without exception, result from immaturity, and are all to be corrected by developing maturity.

➤ Sexual Maturity

Sexual maturity begins with the attitude that sex is not bad in itself, and, when rightly used, will enrich life and add materially to the pattern of enjoyment.

The phrase, "rightly used," is the key to the whole business.

First, "rightly used," means acknowledging the existing restrictions on sexual activity as a necessary and a good thing so long as people are trying to continue the social and economic projects we call civilization. Obviously, to keep out of trouble, sex had best be used within the legal limits, that is to say, only in the married state. This is the one side to maturity — minimizing trouble.

Secondly, "rightly used," means developing the capacity to make the sexual aspect of marriage a satisfactory, complete, and constantly finer experience for husband and wife. This is the other side of maturity — developing the capacity to handle living for maximum enjoyment.

The first meaning of "rightly used" concerns chiefly the person out of wedlock, and the second concerns those who are married.

➤ Handling Sex Before Marriage

As far as a sex program for youth is concerned, an excellent, or even a good, solution does not exist. The best that can be done to help youth is to mobilize a few factors in their behalf that will help tide them over.

The first thing we can do for youth is to be frank about the whole business. It doesn't do to tell these young people they have no problem, or to imply that if they have, it is of their own making. It is best to lay the cards on the table, and admit their elders had the same problem — and for them, as for youth now, the fact is that before marriage, there is no altogether satisfactory answer. Then we should try to make it clear that marriage is a satisfactory answer only if personal qualities of maturity can be developed before they get married.

The second help is not to insist, or even to imply, that the sexual urge should be forced out of mind. Instead, the youth's mind should be given interests and urges, important and lively enough to take up a good portion of his time, interests worthy in their own right of demanding the best the youth has.

Ways to help control the urge. Such urges are the urge to become proficient in a sport, adept and skilled in a handicraft, socially accepted and liked, capable of adding a desirable skill to the community enterprise. Not only will a wealth of such pursuits serve to enable the youth to forget much of the time that he is a sexual animal, but it will also develop the maturities so necessary to his future.

General mental maturity, the capacity to think, is the best step toward sexual maturity. A family which gives the youth a sense of belonging to the family enterprise, an education that gives the youth a keen sense of being a part of the human enterprise, a good mind with generally sound ideas — these are the best measures for sublimating the sex urge to a distinctly secondary level. Such a sublimation of interest and such a development of new urges must be provided, principally by *the family*, and also by the schools, churches, and by youth centers.

The need for youth centers is usually underestimated by our communities, and when the youth centers *are* provided, it is often in too niggardly a fashion. A good youth center in a community, designed to give youth high interests in their off-hours, is the most important organization outside the family. Any community with the interests of its young people truly at heart can much less afford to be without a youth center than it can afford to be without paved streets or a municipal water supply.

A youth center is in the nature of a necessary public utility which only the municipality can provide.

The third help is for adult society to fan the sexual flames

of youth as little as possible. It is entirely laudable to lift
sexuality out of 19th-century prudery, but it is still necessary
that parents, teachers, psychologists, and psychiatrists take
pains to point out to adolescents the dangers of "petting" —
the danger of excessive sex stimulation under conditions
which do not provide for its proper gratification.

One sees high school teenagers, either regrettably pregnant,
or what is almost worse, with wrong emotional habits resulting from petting, which will give them lifelong nervous difficulties. If young people are to be overstimulated by sexy
literature, sexy movies, sexy stories from their elders, plus
the opportunity provided by the family automobile, their
elders should not be surprised when they seek a natural outlet
for their sexual tension. By and large, our society is dealing
youth a wretched hand, and then asking them to play a good
game. The pay-off is apparent in present-day divorce rates
and marital difficulties. For the foolish things people do all
the people pay.

➡ Sexual Maturity in Marriage

Lamentable as poor handling of sex may be in the pre-
marital individual, it is even more lamentable when sex produces clouds of wrong emotions to a married couple, as it
does with great frequency.

In marriage, as in adolescence, general maturity is the best
guarantee of sexual maturity. The same sympathy, understanding, and willingness to cooperate that stamp maturity in
general are absolutely essential if marital sexuality is to be
something other than a source of trouble and internecine
strife. The golden rule of sympathy, understanding, and
kindliness must be the basis of marital sexuality, just as it
must be the basis of mature social ethics. Most people at the
time of marriage have for each other the feeling we call affection. Affection is entirely essential, but unless it is augmented by the golden qualities of sympathy, understanding,
and kindliness on the part of both marital partners, it will

soon be replaced by remorse, disillusionment, bickering, and dissatisfaction.

Sex must be a mutual delight. The sexual relationship in marriage should be a truly cooperative enterprise in which neither wishes to derive pleasure at the expense of the other, and each is more intent in providing the maximum enjoyment for the other rather than for himself. They learn that finding pleasure in each other is a much wider thing than sex, and includes many more things than sex, but in which sex is an important factor.

Creating a mutually enjoyable experience becomes the object of each, and no rules apply except that whatever is done be good and pleasant to both, and enjoyed by both.

When two married people are personally mature together, sexual married life consists of mutual appeal and response, offer and acceptance, enticement, surprise, suspense — all achieved by constantly shifting aggressiveness and passivity, activity and relaxation on the part of each partner.

To two such people the pleasure to each from pleasing the other becomes so intermingled with the pleasure of being pleased and of knowing that the partner is pleased and wants to return the pleasure, that their two personalities become indistinguishable and become truly one through the years.

Each shared pleasure reinforces and builds up a long series of potentially limitless shared experiences of ecstasy. The physical and mental components of pleasure react and enforce each other. Such married partners become more and more indispensable to each other. No marriage can be a successful enterprise in which there is not such a sexual unity.

Egocentricity and selfishness are the childhood arrests that most commonly make a mess of marriage. The only person capable of true affection is the person who can forget himself and his own immediate interest while he places the welfare and interest of someone else foremost. When both husband and wife can do that, they will have no domestic nor sexual trouble.

Assuming now that both marital partners are capable of working for the other's welfare, the stage is set for marital success.

The next quality to maintain in the family between husband and wife, and later between parents and children, is the idea that TODAY, RIGHT NOW, *we are going to be cheerful and pleasant and make living enjoyable.* Quarreling and fighting and bickering are permanently and completely out of the picture because they accomplish exactly nothing. Under *no circumstances* are they justifiable.

The "value" of "blowing your top." There is a school of psychiatrists who think that "blowing one's top" is a good way to work off something bad. This view is held mostly by psychiatrists who cannot control their own tops. There is nothing to it. Blowing one's top serves no good purpose; one blowing more firmly sets the habit for the next blowing. If both husband and wife are given to blowing their tops, something usually cracks sooner or later, such as patience, affection, or the standing invitation to cooperate. Children blow their tops; it is a childish adult who finds it necessary to do so.

Marriage should and can be based on this fundamental assumption: *"We can make life more enjoyable for each other by living together; neither of us has any right to make any moment miserable for the other."* That becomes a perfectly simple, satisfactory, and practical formula if husband and wife each have about a dime's worth of sympathy, understanding and good-will.

In such an atmosphere, the sexual side of marriage becomes a growing experience that constantly makes each more indispensable to the other; sexually their experiences are as cooperative, sympathetic, and understanding as are the other aspects of their life together.

Young married couples should know something about the anatomy and physiology of sex. Ignorance is the only deterrent to human possibilities. When I see young couples going afoul in marriage because their sex life is going sour, along with their other marital enterprises. I refer them to a sensible and concise discussion of sexual relations such as *Sex Manual* by G. Lombard Kelly, M.D.*, which I advise them to read together. Sometimes it is sex that goes sour first in marriage, sometimes it goes sour because everything else has gone sour.

When a marriage gets sour, the first thing for wife and husband to do is for *each of them* to bring cheerfulness and pleasantness back into their attitude toward the other.

KEY POINTS TO REMEMBER IN CHAPTER 11

The individual's sex problem consists in adapting his biological urge to the restrictions imposed by society. Society has imposed the restrictions, but hasn't taken the trouble to teach the individual how to make a mature adjustment. Maturity and emotional stasis in sexual matters boils down to three rules:

- 1. Tell yourself, in no uncertain terms, that in matters of sex you are going to play the game according to the rules. It is easier to keep out of trouble than to get out of it once you are in it. For all-important reasons — legal, moral, social, economic — sex *must* be confined to marriage.

- 2. The successful sublimation of sex in the unmarried person (or in the married wolf) consists in providing the individual with interesting, absorbing, and vigorous activities, and in helping him mature in as many other departments of living as possible.

- 3. Sexual maturity in marriage is dependent on developing the qualities of general maturity, especially sympathy, understanding, unselfishness, cooperativeness and affection.

---

* Published by *The Southern Medical Supply Company*, Augusta, Georgia. This book cannot be secured without a prescription from a doctor.

12.

WHAT TO DO WHEN YOUR WORK IS GIVING YOU THE JITTERS

➤ *The Emotional Stress of Our Industrial System*

Never has the civilized world had the wealth of useful goods and materials that our present-day industrial system provides. That, of course, is a wonderful benefit and help to all the people.

But never has a method of production inflicted on its personnel such a flood of disagreeable emotions as does our present-day industrial system. This, of course, is a primary source of unhappiness and emotionally induced illness for a great many people.

When the industrial system began in England, it was the laborer in the sweat shops who had most of the bad emotions provided by the system. But today it isn't primarily the common laborer, or the white-collar man at the foot of the ladder, who suffers most emotionally because of the system. The greatest victim is the man at the top, or near the top, who masterminds and manages the system. We see here the operation of nature's balance of compensations.

The businessman or the craftsman, before the industrial

age, experienced *few* of the conditions that in today's world produce tense emotional states in corporation executives, vice-presidents, store managers, sales force, assembly line workers and so forth. The incessant competitive business growth, departmental growth, and the pressure of piece work, competitive striving, angling for advancement, low-interest, repetitive jobs, are at once the elements that make the industrial system great, and the elements that give men the emotional jitters and emotionally induced illness.

➡ *The Executive Has Stress*

Werner had come up the hard way in the sales division of a company that makes several well-known, nationally advertised products. The company was old, and didn't amount to much, until one of its new products made a national hit far above anything even the company heads ever expected. From then on, the board of directors wanted to continue putting out "hits."

Werner, by working around the clock for the company, on a small salary, and having no fun for himself or his family, had achieved a good position in the sales division. Then he was placed in charge of sales for a new product that the board hoped would outdo the original "hit." What an opportunity! Werner thought; and there *were* opportunities, including the opportunity never to feel physically well again. The board would call Werner in and show him a comparative chart silhouetting him against some more successful department. The board would ask him for a progress report before the expected time. The board would ask for an explanation of a lower-than-expected sales curve. The board would pound its fist upon the table.

With every new pressure from the board, Werner developed a new pressure in his upper abdomen and chest. After one board meeting he checked his lungs, after another his heart, once his stomach, again his gall bladder.

He was an organ on which the board was playing a dismal tune. Even before Werner was made head of sales, he could never brag that he felt fit as a fiddle. But after his climb to sales manager, with the heat of the board upon him, he became a symphony of complaints, which included a completely equipped indigestion, finally centering around a perennial full-blown ulcer.

I met him the first time on a train. The poor fellow told me of his symptoms, ending with, "And the doctors don't seem to understand it." That last statement usually means the patient doesn't understand it.

Werner worked up a tremendous tension and a diabolical indigestion, trying to bring his product before a reluctant public. Actually, the product he was given by the board to promote was developed 20 years too late. It died a slow, expensive death, and with it, Werner went down in the company, a functional wreck. The effect of the system was exactly the same as if the board had inoculated Werner with tuberculosis. Yet the members of the board considered themselves kindly human beings; they were playing the part of good businessmen, as far as Werner was concerned.

Now take a top-flight success from one of the boards — as a matter of fact, he has been on 22 boards at the same time — Old H———. He worked, he pushed, he pulled, he got there. But getting there meant holding on; holding on meant advancing with a bunch of enterprising young fellows yelping at his heels. There came a steady competitive fight to stem off a reorganization, sleepless nights on which he'd gotten out of bed and walked for blocks, jittery spells when he tried to rest a minute on plane trips he took to secure stockholders' votes; finally a blackout when he hemorrhaged from an ulcer that he had, in his frenzy, tried to ignore. He was a great success — he beat the reorganization — he controlled the stock — he was really a great financier. But as a man he was jumpy, jittery, restless, constantly nursing an ulcer — himself a financial success, and also a financial success for the doctors.

➡ The Half-Way Man Has Stress

Now let us look at some of the lower rungs on the ladder. There is no form of modern business management that is more competitive than being the manager of a chain store. I've known many of these managers — fine fellows, every one of them, smart, honest, hard workers. They had to be to survive the rigid screening process they went through to ascend from clerk to manager. But I have not seen a single one who did not have, in the course of his managership, some form of functional disease.

Bill went farther than any of the others I ever knew; he finally ended as a manager over ten large districts. We X-rayed Bill four times from stem to stern while he was store manager in our town, to assure him that his abdominal pain and constipation were no more serious than his sour stomach and frequent belching. Every advancement, every move to a new city, was punctuated with more X-rays. The last time I saw him in his plush office in Chicago, he was still belching, still eating antacid tablets by the handful, and I could tell from the occasional wince that strolled across his face that he was still having abdominal pain.

Then take Joe. Joe had been a good man in the brass foundry; so good he was made foreman of 27 men. Then his headaches began, and the pain in his neck and in his chest. The men above him wanted output; the men below him wanted to loaf. Between them, Joe was in a vise.

➡ The Laborer's Job Gives Him Stress

Take a look at the lowly assembly lines. Henry left the farm for the glamour of the factory. There he was given the thrill of putting the spark plugs into the engine block as it came down the line. The company speeded up the line. Incidentally, Henry had to speed up too. Then the engineers added two more cylinders; they weren't thinking of Henry.

Henry became more and more ailing. After a necessary leave of absence, he was put on a punch press doing piece work. After two years he broke down again. Now he's back on the farm. He wonders why he ever went to the factory.

A very interesting thing happened in another plant — in one division a dozen men run grinders over sheet metal, producing a terrific piercing noise. I've seen four men from that division with ulcers in the last two years; how many more quit because of stomach trouble, I do not know. You remember that Dr. Hans Selye produced ulcers in dogs by subjecting them to a constant piercing disagreeable noise!

➤ *Worry and Accidents*

It's the worried man in industry who has most of the accidents. Attention to the job is interrupted by a train of thought about a disagreeable problem — possibly trouble with the wife at home — possibly worry over the house mortgage — possibly anxiety over a dozen different things — then zingo! zip! he loses his hand in a press, or a moving rod pierces his arm. Seventy-five per cent of the accidents happen to repeaters.

➤ *The Pressure Is the Same in All Industry*

In every line of modern industry and business, the competitive pressures are the same, probably nowhere greater than in the newspaper game. An editor friend of mine says there is no one on his paper from the editor (himself) on down who doesn't have a few physical complaints. And he adds, "In addition to feeling punk physically, these fellows are fundamentally unhappy, because the pace and the pressures are so great."

➤ *Perhaps Industrial Civilization Is Worth It*

What price modern productive methods? What good is

wealth acquired with a raw stomach? Far better a sweet stomach and a modest living. But where, in modern business-industry, can you find a sweet living without a sour stomach? The tension of bigger and better commercialism ruins almost every job you can pick up.

Modern business and industry is one of the great reasons for the terrific prevalence of the emotionally induced illness of our time. In certain respects the system is a childhood arrest — it is psychologically immature. At a certain age the child is constantly competitive, pitting and matching himself against all comers, striving to beat his fellows, constantly endeavoring to excel. As a person matures, this competitive spirit melts into a cooperative willingess to share with the other fellow, to give rather than to take. Such maturity is frightened off by our present economic Frankenstein.

To be mature in this sense, to act with mature decency when competitive striving calls for selfish pushing ahead, means inevitable failure in the kind of system we have. Anyone who follows such mature principles as noncompetitive cooperation, a desire to be of benefit to human beings as human beings, a feeling for helping people out of difficulties, can be a financial success only by a most miraculous series of accidents.

I know several financial failures, that is to say, men who never succeeded in any business or in any commercial endeavor they ever undertook. Almost without exception, they are among the finest human beings I have ever met.

➡ Still, We've Got to Eat

Nevertheless, we do have to make a living. Maybe you've gotten your functional illness as a direct result of our business-industrial system. You are going to have to continue living in it and being a part of it.

Then (to yourself) play it as a game, something that's a great big lark, something done because it's ENJOYABLE, not a duty. Play it cheerfully and pleasantly, and don't let the trap of competitive striving catch you.

It's barely possible that following this advice, you may never drive a Cadillac, but you'll enjoy eating peanuts and watermelon at a picnic you get to in a rattling good 1937 Chevvy. You may even end up in the poorhouse, but you'll have a good time getting there, and you'll live to sing at the funerals of the poor devils who beat you up the ladder.

A BRIEF SUMMARY OF CHAPTER 12

The industrial system, as we know it in this country, is a wonderful provider of human needs. But unfortunately it is also a great provider of stressing emotions to the people who make it run. Great responsibilities, the constant demand for great effort, and the fight to maintain his gains are common stresses of the top executive. The competitive fight for advancement, with its overshadowing insecurity, is the lot of the man on the way up. Non-creative and low-interest jobs with monotonous repetitions bring a deep form of stress to the laborer.

The only good, long-range answer is that industry must gradually humanize itself, as some portions of industry are already trying to do.

For the individual who is caught in his job, the only answer is to try to sneak enjoyment in through the back door; to make himself as cheerful as possible; and to be upset by the irritations of the job as little as possible. He himself must dictate the level of his emotions, not allow the job to dictate them for him.

In short, the man who is being crushed by industrialism can put the methods you are reading about in this book to good use.

13. MEETING THE AGING YEARS

➡ *Emotional Stress Increases with the Years*

E. I. I. is prevalent at all ages, but it grows more and more prevalent in the declining years of life — the very time an individual should be gliding into a calm, easy harbor, instead of back into the storm. This is true partly because of the conditions and situations that the aging person must try to cope with; on the other hand many people handle age poorly simply because they never handled any part of their lives well. The inability grows larger like a giant snowball toward the end.

This increase with age in the incidence of E. I. I. is a new development in our century. It has come about because aging today is attended by far more stress than ever before in history. For several thousand years the social and economic status of the aged did not change at all; the conditions of the aged in the 4th century, B.C., were practically identical with those of the 19th century, A.D. Today, the status of the aged is very different from what it was 100 years ago, and, in another 50 years, the changes will be even greater.

The important change in our time has been *a tremendous increase in the absolute and relative number of people over 65.* In 1900, one person in 20 was over 65. Today one in 11 is over 65, and by 1980, it will be one in seven.

➡ *"Senility" Is Often E. I. I.*

The functional illnesses of age may be any of those of earlier years, but they tend to assume one similar pattern because the prevalent emotional picture in old age is insecurity (of finances, of health, of the future), apprehension, disappointment, discouragement, and so on.

These emotions, you will remember (Chapter 3), are the ones that stress the pituitary to produce the somatotrophic hormone (STH) with its attending joint, arterial, and kidney effects. In other words, STH effects *are* degenerative effects.

We have no way of judging, as yet, just how much of the degenerative disease of the aged is emotionally induced, but probably a large part of it is. Without the degenerative diseases, which are so chronic and slow and debilitating, the aged person would go along smoothly and fairly vigorously to a happier and more kindly end.

It is important to note that the group of people over 65 is the *only* group whose life expectancy has not increased since 1900. At any age up to 65, you can expect to live longer than an individual of the same age in 1900. But after 65, you cannot expect to live longer than a person of the same age did a hundred years ago. This holds in spite of the fact that practically no old person today dies of pneumonia or other infection, and in spite of the fact that people even with some of the degenerative diseases, such as heart disease, can be carried on for years longer than might have been possible even 20 years ago. It can mean only that degenerative disease has been accelerated in our time, and the cause of the acceleration is an increase in emotional stress.

At first sight, it is hard to believe that much of what we

regard in the aged as natural deterioration is actually E. I. I. But let me give you an example that will illustrate the truth of such a statement.

George W——— illustrated perfectly the way in which the emotions characteristic of old age produce degenerative disease, *and how a change toward the right kind of emotions will produce a reversal of the degenerative changes.* You have to see this sort of thing to believe it.

I was introduced to George by his physician, Dr. K. M. Bowman, a well-known San Francisco psychiatrist. George, at 83, was working on the stage of the theater in the San Francisco Municipal Home for the Aged. He was the stage manager, and he was getting ready for a production the people of the Home were putting on that night. George was as active as a good man of 60, and you could tell he was greatly enjoying his work.

"George," Dr. Bowman said, "Hold out both your hands."

George did. There was a slight tremor in them, especially in the right, but it didn't amount to much.

"How bad did you shake two years ago?," Dr. Bowman asked.

George demonstrated with a terrific wobbling of both hands.

"He isn't exaggerating." Dr. Bowman said.

Then he told me the story. When he had first seen George two years before, George was living with his son and daughter-in-law. He had been bedridden for six months; he shook so hard he had to have help in eating; he was so weak he couldn't take care of his own toilet.

George had been a stage manager on Broadway in his prime. He was a master at his work, one of the best in the business. He had one child, a boy, who moved to the West Coast when he became of age. When George was 48, his wife died. The theater business was declining; some of his shows went sour. For a number of reasons, George began to drink, and he lost the job he had had for 23 years. From then on, he went from job to job, occasionally managing a small, obscure stage, but usually as just a common stagehand.

At 72 he was destitute, and his son sent him enough money to come to San Francisco. There George lived with his son, to whom he had become almost a stranger His habits were not too tidy; his ways were not those of his ʟosts. I suppose at first his son and daughter-in-law had intended to make the old man happy. But the relationship, especially on the part of the daughter-in-law, became one of belligerent and bare tolerance. George knew he wasn't wanted. The city was new to him, he had no friends there; there was no one around the few legitimate theaters who cared to talk to him. So George began to ail; his degeneration became more and more rapid, and it was not too long before he was in bed. They had a doctor once or twice. The doctor called it hardening of the arteries and senile debility.

Then Dr. Bowman chanced to see him. He examined George and said, "We're just finishing a new theater with a fine stage up at the Municipal Home for the Aged, and we need a stage manager from Broadway. I'm going to take you up there."

George was excited, but he didn't think he could ever get out of bed again. His son and daughter-in-law were even more dubious, but secretly they were happy to have him move out of their care.

He was moved in an ambulance, and carted out to the theater stage in a wheelchair. In two weeks he was walking out, and, in another two, he was as active as an old tomcat. He improved rapidly after that.

Around the Home, Dr. Bowman showed me at least eight other people we just chanced to meet who had stories of a reversal of their degenerative disease just as remarkable as George's.

The demonstration that degenerative processes in the aging *can be* the result of *emotional stress* as well as "natural senility" requires a laboratory — like the San Francisco Municipal Home for the Aged. In the average community there is usually little chance to reverse the stressing situation which is producing the degeneration of the aging person.

The San Francisco Municipal Home for the Aged has that *necessary* difference most homes for the aged do not have. One of the best contrasts is afforded by the unimaginative, expensive depositories being built in so many counties for the aged. The central idea of the San Francisco Home is that it is a COMMUNITY of elderly people, run by elderly people. The bookkeeper, the vegetable purchaser, the engineer, the plumber, the stage manager are residents who are old hands at their trade. The Home aims to be self-supporting in a financial way, in a recreational way, and in an essential-service way.

➭ What Getting Old Today Means

Don't think that getting old today is the same kind of thing that getting old was 50 years ago. Times change, and so do the factors that the aging have to contend with.

Financial insecurity. First is the matter of financial security. How well off are you, or how well off are you going to be at the age of 65? With the depreciation of the dollar, which means lower annuities, with the high tax level, with the hesitancy to employ people older than 45, more people than you think are not going to be self-sufficient at the age of 65. The average family today, maintaining the standard of living that everyone has become accustomed to, is just barely able to scrape along, let alone save. We always think that next year we will start to save. The only person who doesn't procrastinate with saving is the financier, or the banker, or the insurance salesman. Don't envy them. They have other problems that give most of them severe functional disease.

One third of the people over 65 have no income whatever of their own, and 75 per cent have an income of less than $1000, including old age assistance. At least there's the Federal old age assistance, you say (if you're under 50). Thank somebody for that. That, at least, is the difference between eating *something* and eating nothing; between sleeping in a bed *somewhere* and sleeping out in the park. Would you (supposing you are 40) like the idea of having to go on "relief"? You can bet your last dollar you won't like it any better when you are 65.

Job insecurity. The last resort of the scoundrel is to suggest, "Why doesn't the old fellow get a job?" The scoundrel doesn't appreciate that in the present labor market it's getting hard for the fellow over 45 to pick up a fresh job.

Here is a man of 60. He is a skilled tool maker, his accident liability is considerably less than a younger man's, his absenteeism will be definitely less, his dependability in a pinch will be greater, he will be less aggressive in fomenting labor trouble. Yet he can't get a job, even though a doctor would pronounce him physically fit. Why can't he, why can't the others of 60 or over — no, let's say 50 or over — get a job so that they might support themselves?

Because, being a vigorous young nation, we worship youth and *slight* (that's a mild term) old age. Old age is regarded as a regrettable incident, necessary (God forbid) for others; an incident which we hope will not be prolonged beyond reason (which isn't long); an incident which will be as troubleless to the younger members of the family as possible (somehow *they* cannot see *themselves* at 65).

The older man doesn't get a job. Some efficiency expert found the younger man more dextrous, turning out more parts for the company. He didn't stop to think that the older man was putting something human into the company; he didn't know that something human in a company would be worth more than lucre. He didn't find out that the company would be still making enough for everyone (including the stockholders and management) to live.

Not being able to make a living or having enough to live on isn't all — it's just the beginning of the troubles which the aging have to take on.

The insecurity of children's indifference. There's the matter, for instance, of changing family sentiment regarding the aged. I can remember the time when "Honor thy father and mother" was taken seriously. If it was the last thing they were able to do, the children felt obliged to see that their aging parents were well cared-for.

Today it is *usual* for children to stand by without emotion (except a sigh of relief) and see their parents placed upon Federal aid; or if the presence of their elders becomes irksome, it is quite satisfactory to see them placed in a nursing home. This has gradually become the attitude that is acceptable to the society in which we live. It is not going to be changed for decades, if ever.

But the truth is that it's terribly hard on the old folks. They remember when these same children had to be fed, had to be protected, required long hours of their time and care. And the compensation is to be set aside as though they had never mattered. For these children they lived. What has it brought them? These children they loved. Now who returns any love? There are plenty of people, don't you fear, who have broken hearts (that is to say, severe pituitary stress) because they have been so damnably let down in their needy years.

More than just the children are at fault. But it isn't only the children. It's *everybody*. Everybody around them regards the aging person as someone who is just in the way impeding progress. Slow on the street; slow getting off of buses; yes, slow to die. Actually and truthfully, the old folks aren't wanted by society. The best indication of that is that we call them a "problem." A problem and the makings of it are not wanted. The kind of county homes we throw them into as a last resort is an indication that we don't really care a great deal for the aged.

Don't think the aged don't sense these attitudes; don't think for a moment that these factors do not have a great deal to do with the health of the aging. That is the point I'm trying to get across. The social solution is evident enough — either children should become old-fashioned enough to care, or society become interested enough to provide adequate community life for those it is now throwing out of society. But that still isn't all that stresses the pituitary to produce STH in the aged.

Fear of ill-health. There's the matter that they don't feel well (suppose it *is* functional) always, always, they fear that complete disability may be just around the corner. The ordinary young person goes into a tailspin when he is told that he needs to be incapacitated for two years. As a matter of fact, it is very seldom that we doctors dare to put it to a patient so simply. Well, now, suppose you have to be afraid, as an elderly patient always has to be afraid, that your age may bring you to your bed tomorrow of a wasting disease you can never be rid of!

It takes a lot of courage in the aged just to act cheerful and never say anything about these fears!

Fear of death. And, too, — you youngsters to whom death is still something that never happens — to the aged (and they think of it, never fear) death is closer at hand than it has ever been. Most every living thing, unless it is very, very miserable, wants to keep on living. And so they think, during those long nights (many are the aged who don't sleep well) of the experience that lies threateningly just ahead. They feel like the Irishman, "If I knew where I was going to die, I'd sure stay away from that damn place." But for them the situation has lost its humor. It's the BIG THING that's just ahead; HOW and WHEN is it going to be?

Loss of friends. But there are all kinds of other sad things for the older person. Their friends who once dropped a cheerful word, their spouse, who once offered a helping hand, their dog, who once wagged his tail, have all gone. Have you ever in the deepening twilight stood out on a lonely sweep of the earth — have you ever felt an awful lonesomeness pulling you down into the soil — a lonesomeness so deep as if to say, "This and only this is all, there is no more?" If you have, you have just a little inkling of how the aged person feels who is *really* alone in the twilight, without a soul to care, or show the least parting affection.

You'd think that after 70, 80, 90 years, one would at least deserve, — if not a band and a celebration — some appreciative recognition from society for having accomplished his feat — staying out of jail, bringing up a family, and just generally carrying on through all the difficulties of the years. But a posthumous text is the best the children and society can wring from hearts that (never fear), too, will grow old.

Poor housing for the aging. Then take another social cause of distress to the aged — the matter of housing. Fifty years ago, two-thirds of our elderly people lived in rural areas. Today, two-thirds live in cities. With this change they have lost the sympathies, friendliness, and neighborliness of the small communities. Today, 50 per cent of our aged have unsatisfactory housing and living arrangements, and a large portion of the other 50 per cent are realizing with dismay that their industrial pensions or other income that had, heretofore, been adequate, no longer cover increased rentals and increased food costs. A person on a Federal pension is expected to feed and house himself on seventy-five dollars a month. Housing on such an income can be only the very worst available, a dreary inhospitable room where one must be ashamed to have visitors.

An age that is dark when it should be golden. And so, old age is for most of the aging in our society the dark age instead of the golden age. For more and more people, the last years mean more and more misery. Those who are now under 55 may think they have their troubles; but when they are 65, they will really know what trouble is.

The troubles of the aging are so acute and so fundamentally devastating, that the miseries of the older people are frequently sending them beyond emotionally induced illness into frank mental derangement. Twenty years ago most of the people in mental institutions were young or middle-aged. The old stayed sane. Today four out of every ten admissions to mental institutions are over 65! The cause?

Simple! The conditions our aged are asked to meet are enough to break men's minds. These patients are often labeled "senile dementias." But don't forget, they are degenerative dementias, emotionally induced. The proportional admissions of the aged to mental institutions has increased considerably faster than the increase in the total number of the aged.

➡ It's Your Problem, Too

Practically every adult living today will live to be 65 and over. In 1925 there were 20 younger people for every person over 65. Today there are only 11 younger for everyone over 65, and in 1975, there will be only 8 younger for everyone older than 65. You see, you are going to get there too! The problem of the aged is not like the problem of India. You will probably never have to live in India, but you will most certainly live to be older than 65. What is to be done about the problems of oldsters?

You are 20 or 25 or 30:

What are you doing about your old age? Now is the best time to start planning.

You are 40 or 45 or into the 50's:

You cannot afford to waste time when time is so precious.

You are 60 or 65:

There is still time to do much — you have a long time to live.

You are in the 70's or 80's:

Contentment, which is something inside and not outside, can still be yours for the trying.

➡ What Will We Do About Old Age?

This:

Whether you are 20 or whether you are 60, the sooner you develop a mature idea of what your program will have to be after you are 65, the happier your old age is going to be.

Maturity in old age means essentially what maturity at any age means — it means that as an individual lives, he enjoys what there is to enjoy, his friends, family, work, spare time, and the wonderful world, and he develops a great kindness and thoughtfulness which enables him to be a giver to all, but especially to those weaker and less fortunate. Finally he is able to compromise and see the other fellow's point of view instead of disagreeing and rearing up into a fight.

➡ Practically, Maturity in Old Age Means This —

If you are young:

1. **Develop emotional stasis now.** We talked about the tough situations our oldsters are faced with. But the most important source of trouble is not any of these. By far the greatest trouble oldsters have — I should say about 75 per cent of their trouble — is that in their upper years their emotional states have at last caught up to them, as emotional states always do by the time we are 65. The reactions a person allowed himself to have when he was 20 become more obvious as a person grows older. Nine times out of ten, the old man "who is just as sweet as he can be" was always a kindly, understanding person. The old lady with an acid tongue and a battle-ax approach to the ordinary incidents of life, was that way when she was 40, and also, though possibly less obviously so, when she was 20. Unless we work on them with conscious thought control, our emotional states in old age are the quintessence of our earlier dispositions with most of the masking flavors filtered off.

So, whether you are 20 or 60 you can still learn kindliness, love for your fellows, cheerfulness, and an eye for the thousands of little enjoyable things about us that cost nothing.

All through life we have a choice — we have the same choice whether we are 20, or 40, or 60, or 80, except that, at 80, we have more strongly established the habit of making the choice in one certain direction. But even at 80 a resolute person can change the habit in his choice. We have the choice between reacting with *equanimity, resignation, courage, determination, and cheerfulness* on the one hand, or with *crabbiness, grumbling, worry, and apprehension* on the other.

The choice is yours — RIGHT NOW.

If a person *realized* that he had a conscious choice between the two ways of reacting to his world, *and he knew the con sequences of taking one or the other path,* he would not hesitate in choosing equanimity, resignation, determination, courage, and cheerfulness. As in many simple truths, the better choice is so obvious it is missed. Somewhere our education should have made it crystal clear that the choice was ours, and that with a flip of our mind a good emotional state was ours, with all the trimmings.

2. **Plan future finances.** Save something regularly to add to retirement income. Cut your present scale of living if you need to. Remember what Thoreau once said, that any event that requires a new outfit is not worth the trouble.

3. **Plan a place to live** when you are advanced in years. Will you have your home or will you have money to pay rent?

4. **Expand your interests** by developing hobbies — gardening, farming, or anything that you can use later when you are done in the office or the shop.

Instead of retiring, start a little trade or a little business, be it ever so small. Get your mind active in new fields; go to night school, take a correspondence course in some new subject. Get acquainted with books.

5. Since you are going to be old some day, **start making people see the problems of the aged** as realistically as you do — they are going to get there too. Above all, help turn sentiment against the type of county old-age homes that are being built in so many states. These are poor solutions to the problems of the aged and the very fact of their existence will, in years to come, forestall a better answer. Throw your opinion

and your efforts toward the establishment of the San Francisco-type of home for the aged, which is a community plan on a community scope. These obviously cannot be built by most counties. They will have to built at the state or Federal level.

If you are already aged:

1. Cooperate with the inevitable and accept gracefully whatever fate may bring.

2. Whenever an old friend departs, seek a new one; life is as empty or full as you make it.

3. Try to be flexible and adaptable in your thinking; avoid prejudice; don't criticize youth for being as they are.

4. Dress neatly; sew up the holes in the old garments very carefully. Retain good, clean manners.

5. Do not dawdle; pursue interests as though you meant business.

6. Above all, keep the disposition pleasant and cheerful. Greet people with a smile and a kind word. Don't gripe except when no one else can hear you, and when you can't hear yourself.

7. Never let yourself know how tired you are. Just sit down for a while, telling yourself that doing so was what you had in mind, anyway.

8. Don't worry about dying. Everyone who lived before you stood it.

A SUMMARY OF CHAPTER 13

Instead of being a Golden Age, the sixties, the seventies, and eighties are an age of increased emotional stress owing to financial insecurity, job insecurity, children's indifference, the fear of ill health, fear of death, the loss of friends, poor housing, and general public indifference. Much of what is regarded as senile degenerative disease is actually emotionally induced illness, in which STH factors are prominent.

If you are young, prepare for age by developing emotional stasis, that is to say, a happy disposition — NOW. Plan future finances and a place to live when you are old. Develop new active interests, against the time when your job runs out.

If you are already aged, you can produce contentment inside, even if there isn't any reason for it outside. Cooperate with the inevitable; find a new friend when an old one leaves. Stay flexible and adaptable in your thinking. Do not criticize youth. Dress neatly. Keep that disposition pleasant; greet people with a smile. Sit down when you must, but don't let yourself know how tired you are. And as for death — didn't everyone before you stand it?

14.

THE FULFILLMENT OF
YOUR SIX BASIC NEEDS

There are some people with E. I. I. who are unaware of any emotions that might be responsible for their illness. These people frequently have fundamental emotions of a wrong variety because their *basic psychological needs* are not being filled.

The ordinary human being, like you and me, has six basic instinctive needs — six psychological WANTS — things that he feels deeply inside himself he must have. If one of these needs is not filled, a deep-seated restlessness is produced, a vague unrequited longing, and an undercurrent of disappointment that colors every minute of the day and night

Such an individual may be adapting himself very well, otherwise, to his environment, managing to put up a cheerful pleasant front; but deep down inside, there is a great gnawing longing because one or more of his psychological needs is only an empty yawning sore of misery.

➡ 1. *The First of These Basic Needs Is the Need for Love*

Everyone (even the person who seems to hate everybody
182

else) has an inner desire and need for love — he wants to receive the affection and high regard of at least one other human being. Receiving such affection makes us feel important and valuable; it makes us feel that we have a place in the order of people and things.

The proper fulfillment of this need adds a glow of warmth, richness, and beauty to what is otherwise very dull living. If there is no love from anyone, no high regard from a single other soul, a deep vacuum is made in a person into which are sucked the emotions of distress, longing, lonesomeness, and, eventually, social hostility. And these unhealthy emotions are present constantly, day and night, tainting the fundamental background of living.

This lack may begin in childhood. There are many unfortunate people who feel the sting of the lack of affection from early childhood on, because they have the bad luck to have been born into a family where real affection simply does not exist. Mother and father wage a continual cold war against each other, with periods when the war gets pretty hot and the air is filled with angry words, with, perhaps, a dish or two for punctuation. What they can't take out on each other, the parents take out on the children.

The children, learning by imitation, imagine that constant bickering, quarreling, spite, and hatred are the stuff that all life is made of; so sisters and brothers return blow for blow. Everyone feels alone, hunted, exploited, uncomfortable, and on the defensive. These boys and girls may get quite old, or may go all the way through life, without ever getting the idea that there is such a thing as affection, or that there are human beings capable of it. But the psychological need for it is present, and these people have a restlessness, and a yearning, for something they haven't got. Basically, they are very unhappy.

The odd and tragic thing is that they don't consciously realize it and, of course, they don't know that it is lack of affection that underlies their restlessness.

This sort of thing isn't at all uncommon. It often shows its effects (which are functional disease and gross unhappiness) in some of the best families.

Verna was a beautiful girl whose mother died when she was a baby. Her father, who showed very little affection for her at any time, put the girl in an orphanage where she found more abuse and psychological torment than affection. At the age of 15, she met Eugene, an only child and a wealthy boy, with a very protective and selfish mother.

Eugene was captivated more by Verna's sexual attractiveness than anything else, and for the first (and only) time in his life, he did something his mother did not want him to do — he eloped with Verna. Verna had received no affection in the orphanage and she received less as the wife of Eugene. Eugene was too selfish, too self-centered and dependent on his mother to be capable of affection for Verna. Eugene's mother, who always lived just a few blocks away, resented Verna's position with her son and did her best to hold Eugene and turn him against Verna in every way she could.

For years this went on. When children came, the mother worked on them to turn them against Verna; in this she succeeded to the point where a 16-year-old daughter repeatedly told Verna, "I hate you!" The need for affection wasn't the only need that went empty in Verna; some of the others that we are going to talk about, likewise, were empty gulfs of despair. Verna experienced years of functional disease which grew gradually to the point of complete disability. When the cause of her illness was explained to a much-doubting husband and mother-in-law, they went through the outward appearance of affection. But wise Verna sensed this as a sham. The only thing that could have altered the situation would have been for Verna to start life all over. It was only with great difficulty and self-discipline that Verna began to feel a sense of value in the returned good-will of other people when she went into Red Cross work on an all-out scale.

Even worse than Verna's situation is the situation of a girl who has been brought up in an affectionate family atmosphere and then finds herself married to a man who is capable of about as much affection as a cold blob of cottage cheese. These husbands (and there are a lot of them) forget their wives are human beings with human wants and feelings.

These chaps have little idea that there are such things as human wants and feelings — outside their own. They have a childhood arrest in certain essential compartments of their personalities. If they are capable of any affection, they never show their wives the capacity. After all, it would be easy for the big lugs to show the little woman some affection in many little ways every day. A hug, a kiss, a pleasantry, a compliment on her appearance, or an appreciation of a meal, would put a few blooms in the arid desert that such a woman, unfortunately, inhabits.

It finally serves the big fool right when he has to pay a long, hard medical bill for functional illness of which he is the cause. But this, too, he turns against the wife, blaming her for the sickness his immature stupidity produced. Men like this are one of the big reasons for functional illness in married women.

Sexual love is basically important. The thing we call love, the kind of thing we mean by affection, is a complex thing composed of various parts, and part of this basic need for love is the basic need for sexual love. In any marriage, conjugal affection is intimately bound with sexual affection. A marriage can seldom be unified, affectionate, and mutually satisfactory if the sexual experience between the partners is not unified, affectionate, and mutually satisfactory.

If, for one reason or another, sexual love never develops in a marriage, or fades away and disappears, one or both of the married couple becomes restless, dissatisfied, grumbly, irritable, and complaining. The functional disease produced by this kind of a situation is often hard to treat because the patient would rather not tell about the trouble; consequently it can never be remedied. Sometimes this kind of trouble is hard to remedy anyway. But this type of trouble produces some very odd results.

For instance, Mrs. T—— had a severe fibrositis of the lower back, so severe that she went to many clinics and many hospitals. The usual treatment did her very little good.

Mrs. T—— was a career woman. Both she and her husband held important and responsible positions that took precedence over their home life. After their day's work, they came to a home (managed by a housekeeper) used only for meals or for social entertainment. Their sexual life gradually grew thinner and more disinterested, partly because of Mrs. T——'s tendency to deprecate sexuality in favor of her career, and finally because Mr. T—— found more satisfaction in a secret mistress.

At first the decreasing sexual atmosphere of their marriage was welcomed by Mrs. T——. Then she developed fibrositis, which on the surface had nothing to do with Mrs. T——'s womanliness. But then she, too, was catapulted into the arms of a lover, and for the first time in her life experienced sexual satisfaction. The remarkable thing was that her fibrositis disappeared *at once*.

Because of her career position, and also because of a profound feeling of guilt, Mrs. T—— periodically tried to deny herself to her lover. With each of these episodes, the fibrositis returned, only to disappear when this illicit love was allowed again into her life.

In many other ways, sexual incompatibility or unhappiness in marriage is the primary cause of functional disease in husband or wife, or both.

The old people must be loved, too. A group of people who commonly suffer from the need of love and affection are the aged, who must walk more and more alone as those whom they loved, and those who loved them, are taken away by the robber, death. An old man loses his wife, the only person who showed him affection, and finds in her place a daughter-in-law, who shows him in many little open or half-hidden ways that he belongs in the category of a "necessary-care which-we-will-have-to-tolerate." And so the last of life, for which the first was made, becomes a toasting on a spit turned by a mean wench, assisted by her children, silently aided by the unfeeling attitude of the man's own son. A great deal of what in older people appears superficially to be degenerative disease characteristic of old age is in fact functional disease, the result of the lonesomeness, futility, despair, and sadness that have become the closest companions of their nights and days.

➤ 2. *Your Second Basic Need Is the Need for Security*

Freud said that man wants most of all to be loved. Adler, that he wants most of all to be significant. Jung, that he wants security. All three are valid; man is complex and needs many things.

You feel secure if — and only if — there is enough income to buy at least the necessities of life now and in years to come, if your right to life is protected from irresponsible fiends and egomaniacal tyrants by a just government, if you are relatively sure that you will not be struck down by a devastating disease or catastrophe, if you have about you people you know will help you through a deal of trouble.

Because *complete* security is an impossible thing, many worry warts defeat an otherwise secure state by worrying over the insecurity of security. They worry about cancer, and experience, thereby, more agony than death, again and again. To them, government policies spell their certain ruin 30 years hence. They are sure that disaster, in one of its endless forms, is always around the corner.

Such people, of course, never know a feeling of security. Because of continual insecurity, they lead miserable lives, mentally and physically. They became racked with functional disease. The trouble with people like these is obvious; they are always worrying right out in plain sight before the entire world.

But many people who *are* in insecure positions never show it outwardly, and very often even minimize their insecurity to themselves. Yet down beneath the surface of moment-to-moment emotions, they have a deep feeling of insecurity, felt through its physical manifestations.

An executive may feel an insecurity in regard to his position because capable younger men are coming up and pushing at his heels. A man may feel insecure about life itself — the boy in battle, the Jew in Nazi Germany, the anti-communist in Soviet Russia. There may be the insecurity felt by a woman whose husband wants a divorce. There may be the insecurity felt by the boy who is the target of bullies in a boarding school. There is the insecurity felt by a man in any kind of a serious jam.

There are hundreds or, perhaps, thousands of varieties of insecurity this world can concoct for those who live in it. Even though we keep them in the background of our thinking, these insecurities can become the type of monotonous repetitions of unpleasant emotions that lead to functional disease.

One of the common ingredients that people discover in old age is a feeling of insecurity. They need to fear ill health, particularly disabling illness. Many need to fear financial insecurity. Many feel insecure as to what the end of life may bring them. There is the inevitable feeling of insecurity at losing loved ones whom they depended upon for certain assistance and qualities of life.

So, to a lack of affection many aged people must add lack of security. At the time when life should be gentle and kind, it becomes cruel and forbidding. When the race is nearing the end and a fellow is coming down the homestretch, there should be the cheering of the audience along the way; instead there is the jeering of the insensitive, and the interrogation of the welfare department.

The types of emotion that these situations saddle upon the elderly persons are those emotions that stress the pituitary production of STH. The chronic STH effects are essentially those of degeneration of the kidneys, the arteries, and the organs, in general, as you saw in Chapter 4. Thus it is that degenerative changes are accelerated by the old person's adverse situations. If the type of emotion in such individuals is changed by fulfilling the basic needs in which they have been deficient, such as the needs for love and security, the processes of degeneration are reversed to such a degree that the individual seems to become years younger.

Many families are made to feel the pangs of insecurity because of a nonsupporting husband; whether the lack of support stems from alcoholism, laziness, or bad luck alters only the intensity of the emotions, not their essential color. The impending loss of home, property, and prestige add up to headaches, disturbances of the gastrointestinal system, and a host of other functional effects.

➤ 3. *The Third Basic Need Is the Need for Creative Expression*

The child building with blocks, the housewife making a set of curtains, the financier planning a new holding corporation, the girl writing poetry, the carpenter building a house — all have the very satisfying feeling that out of raw materials they are creating something new.

No one, including you and me, has fundamental happiness if he is not being constructive either in his leisure hours or in his work. It is natural for everyone to identify himself with the world of human beings and to feel that he is assuming a part in that world. The universal urge toward creative expression is a vague kind of restlessness that becomes more and more unpleasant and disturbing if it is not put into action. But when it is put into action, there is the accompanying thrill – a sort of mental breathlessness, and an inward joy of *doing* and *creating*.

Creative activity must not be thwarted. There is probably no frustration greater than a thwarted person with an intense desire for major creation. There was Ethel, for instance, whom I saw because of a functional illness she developed because her desire for creation was nipped in the bud by an unthinking family.

Ethel married Roger. They were both fine people with excellent families behind them. Through high school and college, Ethel had built up plans of the kind of home and the kind of family she wanted to raise. At the time of their marriage, economic conditions in the country were bad, and Roger's parents invited the newlyweds to live on the first floor of their own home. They moved to the second floor. Ethel's mother-in-law was a considerate, kind individual who wished to be tactful and kind to Ethel. She cautiously and carefully suggested to Ethel that she might do a certain thing in such and such a way. Ethel was truly grateful for the tip and followed the suggestion. The mother-in-law was encouraged, by Ethel's enthusiasm, to make more suggestions.

As Ethel's children came, the mother-in-law took a more and more active hand. Ethel had an inner, unexpressed feeling that she had in fact become a member of Roger's family and was rearing no new family, was creating no home of her own. Her dreams were dissolving into nothing. Worse still, she couldn't get out of her predicament without being rude in the extreme and making life miserable for all of them. Ethel grew gradually more frustrated and began more and more to suffer ill health. This was an additional indication to the mother-in-law that her help was needed. The mother-in-law was, in fact, the mother of both families; Ethel was a dependent child. And Ethel became quite ill.

Because Roger and his parents were intelligent people, the doctor could at last make them see Ethel's predicament; they could be shown that Ethel needed above all to be the Ethel she had always hoped to be; she needed to be allowed to create her own home and her own family. Ethel and Roger moved away by themselves in a new home they planned together. Ethel recovered.

There are many people just as deeply upset, just as frustrated as Ethel, because they have been unable to follow an urge to do or to create certain things, an urge they may have felt since childhood. These people may appear to be cheerful people on the surface, but the deeper color of their emotions is anything but happy — their thwarted drives end in restless, unrequited yearning, anxiety, discouragement, and finally, perhaps, a loss of self-esteem.

➤ 4. *The Fourth Need Is the Need for Recognition*

There is in everyone the need to feel that he and his efforts are being appreciated — appreciated by those for whom we strive.

Everyone needs to be regarded by *someone* as being of *some* importance, and doing *something* that is of *some* good.

It often happens that a man may leave a perfectly good position because he feels that his efforts are not being properly appreciated. He resents the fact that although he worked above the call of duty and did an extraordinarily good job, none of his superiors or equals showed any indication of having recognized it. His need for recognition is given a severe blow. He leaves.

The unthanked home-maker. But consider the housewife. Actually, from a standpoint of sheer dreariness and the amount of time spent on the job, she has the toughest job there is. But most of our housewives never receive a word of recognition from one year's end to the other. They, and their washing and ironing, come to be taken as a matter of course by their husbands and children. The meals are accepted in the same silent air of "after all, we have this coming." Everyone assumes that the house cleans itself, that the things they drop pick themselves up, that clean clothes get into the closets automatically, that the comforts of home just naturally exist without anyone's skillful touch.

This lack of recognition for a difficult job, this thankless ness, goes a long way to make homemaking the world's toughest job. The husband quits his job because of lack of recognition, but the housewife doesn't quit hers. But she feels all the more keenly the disappointment at the lack of recognition. Much of the tiredness that goes with constant housework rises directly out of the lack of recognition the housewife receives. Her tiredness is the tiredness of a human being who is being relegated to the position of a lifeless, meaningless drudge.

The unthanked oldster. Again in old age, there is this matter of lack of recognition.

Most of the recognition for his work, or recognition of him as an individual, goes out of an older person's life with the death of his friends. An important element in what we mean by friendship is the trading of mutual recognition. A man who has no friends can fill his need for recognition only by sheer capacity, and that avenue is no longer open to the elder who is denied a job at his old trade. The people who remain surrounding the elder regard age as incapacity, and generally do not regard the old as worthy of respect because they are old. Especially when he is poor, the elder is regarded as a social inconvenience. If he is rich, he becomes an exploitable opportunity. In place of recognition, the aged person is treated as a failure, a burned-out being who is about to be flicked away. A person who lived courageously and well, whose earlier actions benefited the younger generation who are now critical, is often ushered out coldly and unsympathetically, under a hail of spiritual, if not physical, stones. Gone the recognition; gone the acclaim; just an old man no one really wants. Such a crying need of recognition brings emotions that hasten the end.

Appreciate your child, but don't spoil him. At the beginning of life, too, recognition is important — just as important as love. The intelligent, advanced child is apt to be showered with too much recognition — he may be buried in it so that he can never get his head out into the clear and really evaluate himself for what he is, and forever after he lives under the handicap of too high an opinion of himself.

On the other hand, the slow and awkward child's feeling of recognition may be very negligible. He tries in his halting imperfect way to do something that might bring a bit of the recognition which he, like everyone else, longs for. But instead, the reactions of those around him make him feel that his efforts belong in the failure class. He feels that he does not measure up to his brothers or sisters. All the attention he receives is on the disciplinary level. Compliments rarely come his way. He develops an increasing sense of incompetence. The important element of self-esteem gradually leaves him, perhaps never to return. He is always miserable and restless. He may seek even the kind of recognition that the doer of bad deeds receives. He becomes a lost cause because his need for recognition is a lost cause.

➤ 5. *The Fifth Need Is the Need for New Experiences*

A human being cannot be kept in a dull monotonous routine without developing a monotonous repetition of unpleasant emotions, and functional disease with it. Any kind of a job, long continued, carries with it a certain amount of monotony. But the most monotonous job can be made bearable by the thought of a new experience that lies ahead. As one housewife said, "I'd scream if I didn't have that trip to the Black Hills next month to look forward to."

It's an emotionally bad day that starts without the hope or expectancy of a single lift. Even a trip to the meat market might be called a lift; so might an airy conversation, or an interesting person.

Here again the housewife is decidedly in a more unfortunate position. The average day offers more variations and opportunities for new experiences for the male of the species. He goes outside the house and outside the neighborhood to work, meets and talks to people, and his work itself may hold interesting variations. These ready opportunities for new experiences are not available to his wife.

Probably the best example I have seen of how a dearth of

new experiences can produce severe functional disease was Mrs. S——. She was only 26 when I first saw her. She was staying with her mother because she had been sick abed almost three months. Whenever Mrs. S—— tried to get up, she became so dizzy and faint she had to go back to bed. She was obviously hyperventilating. I remember when the call first came to see her. I was occupied, and I sent a fourth-year medical student who was a preceptee in my office.

He returned all aglow, "Oh, boy, do I have a dandy hyperventilator for your clinic!" The lad was a smart student. The several doctors, who up to that time had cared for Mrs. S——, had labeled her illness variously as "anemia," "female trouble," and even "heart disease," so that, in addition to being discouraged, she was also confused.

Since childhood, Mrs. S—— had been an eminently normal sort of person — which means also that she had the normal fulfillment of her basic needs. She married during World War II and soon had two children. When her husband left the Army, he took a job trucking bread from a central distributing station to outlying towns. He left home at two o'clock in the morning and got back at noon. Houses were at a premium but they finally found one that had the advantage of a low rent. The house was six miles from the nearest town, a desolate, dull-green house, set on a desolate, rocky, treeless hilltop. There, in that dismally awful setting, with no neighbors, with only shabby, poorly furnished rooms, Mrs. S—— tried hard and desperately to make a livable home and bring up the children in a happy frame of mind.

Because of the husband's need for sleep, and because of the small children, the couple found it impossible to go out evenings. Besides, there was nothing convenient to go to. After her husband left in the wee early hours, Mrs. S—— felt afraid to be alone with the children in that desolate place. A restless, questionable watch dog offered poor solace. The brown, weathered rocks outside added a dismal dreary note during the day.

Had the husband had a dime's worth of understanding, five cents' worth of sympathy, and two cents' worth of good intentions, he might have sensed what the situation meant for his wife. He made *his* bread rounds, joked with the other truckers and workmen, *saw* things and *did* things. Mrs. S—— couldn't even leave the place because Mr. S—— had to take the car to work.

He was surprised and disgruntled as his wife became increasingly more complaining and sick. Her increasingly long stays with her mother he regarded as depriving him of a home he was rightfully entitled to. He criticized her for the medical expense she was creating. Finally, after the medical student had discovered Mrs. S——'s true illness, Mr. S—— thought the doctor's explanation was an unrealistic figment of the imagination.

But later on, Mr. S—— did develop more of an appreciation for his wife's needs when he found that after treatment she was again a functionally valuable housewife who could get his meals and wash his clothes. She improved even more after he had moved her to a nice little place in an attractive little town where she had a tree in the yard, pleasant neighbors, and a sandbox for the children. It was little enough.

But, as I said, Mrs. S—— was a normal person — she had a good power of adjustment. It had been the utter impossibility of new experiences (which a sensitive, life-loving girl like Mrs. S—— needs) plus, of course, the lack of security, the absence of affection, and the depressing effects of that awful environment, that had tossed her into bed for three long months. But now she is doing fine.

➡ ## 6. *The Sixth Basic Need Is Self-Esteem*

In spite of disappointments, in spite of the little or big personal failures that a person experiences through life, most everyone, nevertheless, manages to think sufficiently well of himself to be encouraged to go ahead. His actual capacities may be ever so minute, his deficiencies may (to others) far overshadow his insignificant good qualities, but he himself is able to find some field for personal satisfaction — at least a rebuttal against criticism, supporting it with an injustice complex.

A person who is fired from a job he thought he was holding down well, or a person who is "told off" by someone whose good-will he assumed, or a person who loses, by some catastrophe, all he has been working for, feels afterward as though there were nothing left, he feels the utter emptiness of failure; he is done up. But after a little time, his assurance, his feeling that he is worth something after all, gradually returns, and though it may be nicked and chipped a bit, his self-esteem is back. He hardly notices the nicks.

But there are many people who lose *every* vestige of self-esteem; they look upon themselves as failures in every respect; there is nothing more to do or to try. They feel they have no place in the world, no worth, no importance, no ability, no judgment, no future, no past except guilt and failure. There is no bottom to the despair these people feel. They are the most miserable, the sickest, and the most deplorable of all human beings. Such a condition in which *all* self-esteem is gone is called a depressive state. The sheer hopelessness of it all, hour after hour, may finally bring a fling of desperate bravado; this is known as a *manic-depressive state*.

Two types of person prone to depression. Two types of people are most apt to lose their self-esteem and have depressive states. One type is the person with a great abundance of self-confidence and esteem without much in the way of abilities to back it up. The other is the person who starts out with a strong inferiority complex in youth, never rises above it, and finally succumbs to a series of failures.

Depressions can occur anytime during life, but are most common after middle life, about the time when one looks back and recoils from the obvious fact that one's accomplishments and achievements have nowhere measured up to early plans and hopes. This alone will not bring on the depression, but if there is added a set-back or two, preventable or un-preventable, what is left of self-esteem begins to vaporize.

John Doe was always a confident fellow who bragged rather easily. He was always ready to criticize the other fellow's political or religious views and "set him straight." This made him somewhat of an irritation in any office, particularly to the boss whose abilities John Doe regarded as far lower than his. At forty, John Doe stormed out of the office one day. He had quit! What was more, he had put the boss in his place. Work at that time was easy to get, and J. D. joined a much larger company where he figured his abilities would be recognized and amply rewarded.

But he was never advanced. His politics grew very nasty. He began to be sharp to everyone and anyone. And one day, when he was 56, he was calmly told his services were no longer necessary. This time a job was much harder to find, and before he found one, he became truly alarmed that possibly another job was not to be had. He was on his new job only two months when he was laid off. His wife, who had never been too easy to live with, berated him day and night.

John was at last completely flattened out. All that he thought he was, he now recognized as a mistake; everything he had prided himself on was now a delusion; the things he had always dreamed of being and doing had melted away. The only future lay with the welfare department. John Doe went into a severe depression and was institutionalized at the expense of the state.

There are all sorts of variations on that theme. Sometimes the failure of the individual is unquestionable, but sometimes the failure is not nearly so great as the victim imagines it is.

What happens in either case is that the person does not have enough self-confidence to go on or to do anything. He is in a state of being personally whipped.

The loss of this sixth psychological need has more immediate and apparent effects than does the lack of any of the other basic needs. The others lead eventually to an agitated feeling of vague anxiety and unrest. The loss of self-esteem is characterized by the depressive state.

Gradually the feeling of complete failure wears off, and after months or years, the person again acquires enough self-esteem to become useful to himself and others.

If a person who is developing a depression can put into action the program of conscious thought-control, which we are outlining in these chapters, he can avert his depression. Once a classical depression has developed, there are only two things that can be done to help the patient: take care of him and wait until the depression wears off naturally, or give the patient electroshock therapy, which snaps him out of it in two or three weeks. The alternative to this is, of course, to exercise conscious thought-control and keep yourself out of a dangerous depression.

➦ What to Do About Your Basic Needs

Review for yourself the presence or absence in your life of these six basic psychological needs. Ask yourself: **Do I in my private world:**

- 1. Receive the *love* of others, or am I a lone, unwanted individual;
- 2. Have *security*, or am I afraid of my finances, my job, my social status, my legal status;
- 3. Exercise *creative expression* in my work, in my hobbies, or in any other way;
- 4. Receive the *recognition* of any of my fellow men;
- 5. Have the possibility of *new experiences*, or am I an old fossil in a deep rut;
- 6. Have my own *self-esteem*, or am I going down in my own estimation?

You might as well be frank, candid, and objective in your answers — it is yourself you are dealing with.

1. If you are situated somewhat like Verna, and there is

no one in your world who really cares a penny's worth about you, the best compensation is to give your love to those about you, and do for them as you would like to be done by. Part of maturity, you will remember, is to have the giving rather than the receiving attitude. It becomes a great satisfaction to love and do good for the people around you who do not deserve or expect it.

2. If it's **security** you lack, decide what you are going to do about it and then quit turning it over and over in your mind. If you cannot do anything to increase your security, there is no use adding worry to it; it's already bad enough. Remember how William, King of Living, handled insecurity? You might re-read Chapter 8.

3. If it's **creative expression** you lack; if you feel you are not making or creating *anything*, that you are just a machine for menial chores, get busy and don't let it eat you any longer. Try doing something you have always hankered to do; try it on your own; or go to the nearest vocational school and pick up a creative art. You might as well start to live!

4. If it's **recognition** that you yearn for, quit yearning; accept the compensation of knowing that you are doing as good a job *for other people* as you possibly can. Give them the recognition instead.

It could be, madam, that if your husband reads this the big goof might give you a little recognition tomorrow by saying, "It is a wonderfully good dinner, my darling!" It would feel good, wouldn't it? But even if you get no recognition from him, you tell him, "You look fine and nice this morning, Fred! I've got a swell-looking man!" He'll like that, and your recognition of him will help you almost as much. Maybe someday he'll give some of it back.

5. If you've become a drudge, caught tight in dull routine, by all means, bust out into some new experience. You should be looking ahead and planning a new experience all the time. Buy something; do something, something exciting; join something; go somewhere. Off with you, this minute, into planning a new experience!

6. If your self-esteem has been jolted lately, smooth yourself with humility. Don't try to be, don't think yourself as being, too much. Just an ordinary person. There have been lots of them — many more of that kind than any other. Lincoln was a plain person, with humility, just like you. Then smile! Put conscious thought control into action to substitute equanimity, courage, determination, and cheerfulness for those stress emotions of failure, disappointment, futility. You are just as good as I am; and we are just as good as they are, God bless them!

THE IMPORTANT POINTS TO REMEMBER
IN CHAPTER 14

There are six basic psychological needs in every person. If a person lacks any one of them in his life, he will be basically unhappy, tense, and restless without knowing why. These needs are the need for **affection, security, creative expression, recognition, new experiences, and self-esteem.**

- If you lack love and affection from others —
  Give more than your share of love and affection to others.
- If you lack security —
  There is no use adding worry to a bad situation; run the emotionally healthy flags up on your masthead.
- If you lack creative expression —
  Go to it, nothing is holding you.
- If you lack recognition —
  Give recognition to other people instead; some of it will come back.
- If you lack new experiences —
  Go out and get them; be planning something all the time.
- If you have lost your self-esteem —
  Remember this: you are just as good as I am, you and I are just as good as they are, God bless them.

15.

HERE IS YOUR FINAL BLUEPRINT

➡ The Choice Is Yours

Practice thought control. When you catch yourself starting a thought that will produce a stressing emotion like worry, anxiety, fear, apprehension, discouragement, or the like, STOP IT, and substitute thinking that brings a healthy emotion, like equanimity, resignation, courage, determination, and ˍheerfulness.

➡ Keep This Always in Mind:

The key thought: Carry this idea every minute of every day: *I am going to keep my attitude and thinking calm and cheerful* — RIGHT NOW.

➡ Handle Life This Way:

When the going is good: Tell yourself life is good, and allow yourself the delightful feeling of being happy.

When the going gets rough: 1. Stay outwardly as cheerful and as pleasant as you possibly can. Lighten an awkward situation with a lift of humor, with kindness, or a bit of a smile.

2. Avoid running your misfortune through your mind like a repeating phonograph record. Above all, do not let yourself get irritated, upset, hysterical, or self-pitying.

3. Try to turn every defeat into a moral victory.

4. Run these flags up on your masthead and *keep them flying*:

- **Equanimity** ("Let's stay calm.")
- **Resignation** ("Let's accept this setback gracefully.")
- **Courage** ("I can take all this and more.")
- **Determination** ("I'll turn this defeat into victory.")
- **Cheerfulness** ("See, I'm coming up.")
- **Pleasantness** ("I still have goodwill toward men.")

➡ *Important Areas in Living to Watch*

- **Keep life simple.**
- **Avoid watching for a knock in your motor.**
- **Like work.**
- **Have a good hobby.**
- **Learn to be satisfied.**
- **Like people.**
- **Say the cheerful, pleasant thing.**
- **Turn the defeats of adversity into victory.**
- **Meet your problems with decision**

- Concentrate on making the present moment an emotional success.
- Always be planning something.
- Say "Nuts" to irritations.

➡ Make Your Family an Asset Rather Than a Liability

Put These Things into the Family:

- Simplicity in living, and simplicity in enjoyment.
- The idea of the family enterprise.
- The idea that the family is part of the human enterprise.
- The attitude of turning defeat into victory.
- An atmosphere of affection, mutual respect and regard.
- A general tone of kindly cheerfulness.
- Reasonable, firm, yet pleasant discipline.
- A feeling of mutual confidence and security.
- An atmosphere of enjoyment — right now.

➡ Control Your Sex Urge Rather Than Having It Control You

- **If you are unmarried:** Sublimate your energies into interesting, absorbing, and vigorous activities, and develop your general maturity.

- **If you are married:** Every relation between you and your wife, or husband, and this includes the sexual relation, needs to be mature, that is to say, sympathetic, understanding, unselfish, cooperative, and affectionate.

- **In any case:** Be content to keep sexuality within the accepted bounds. It is easier to stay out of trouble than to get out of it once you get into it.

➡ *Fill Up Your Own Unfulfilled Basic Needs*

Here Is How:

- If you lack love and affection from others —
  Give more than your share of love and affection to other human beings.

- If you lack security —
  There is no use adding worry to a bad situation; run the emotionally healthy flags up on your masthead.

- If you lack creative expression —
  Go to it, nothing is holding you.

- If you lack recognition —
  Give recognition to other people instead; some of it will come back.

- If you need new experiences —
  Go and get them; be planning something all the time.

- If you have lost your self-esteem —
  Remember this: you are just as good as I am; you and I are just as good as they are, God bless them.

➡ *This Blueprint Leads to Maturity*

By following the blueprint (and the choice is yours) you will be developing maturity and emotional stasis.

Maturity Is This:

- *Responsibility* and *independence*, instead of dependence.

- A *giving* rather than a *receiving* attitude.

- *Cooperativeness* and a *feeling for the human enterprise*, instead of egoism and competitiveness.

- *Gentleness, kindliness,* and *good-will,* instead of hostile aggressiveness, anger, hate, cruelty and belligerence

- The ability to distinguish *fact* from fancy.
- *Flexibility* and *adaptability*, instead of awkward and stubborn resistance to changes dictated by fate, fortune, and intelligence.

➤ Good Living Is Yours

If you are going to limp through year after year of anxious, troubled misery, 100 years, or 75, or even 50, is an interminable hell on earth; the shorter life is, under such conditions, the better; none at all would be best.

But once you learn the trick of striding along, eyes calm with equanimity; head up with determination; chest out with courage; a pleasant word for fellow-travelers, and resignation on meeting rocky rough roads, your years will beg repetition, and your living will be a fascinating enterprise that you would welcome for a hundred years.

The choice of whether to limp or to stride is yours — RIGHT NOW.

A WORD TO THE
PROFESSIONAL READER

The physician who prescribes this book for his patient, or the teacher who is interested in "total" education, may wish to know more about the psychological concepts underlying my method of treating emotionally induced illness.

➡️ *The Basic Psychological Concept in the Method*

The basic psychological concept of the method of treatment presented in this book is the *learning-maturity concept*. Simply stated, this means that emotional stress is the result of miseducation, or lack of proper education, and that emotional stasis can be achieved by *learning* the qualities that comprise *maturity*. Stress is bound to arise in an immature person because he is trying to handle adult situations and problems with primitive and childish techniques. The learning-maturity concept has gradually been emerging from the constantly boiling cauldron of psychiatric and psychological thinking. This concept is the direct antithesis of Freudian psychiatry, which has been oriented by the concept that emotional stress is conditioned early in life by an unacceptable experience that is relegated to the dusky murkiness of the subconscious, where it preys on the host forevermore.

The learning-maturity concept further implies that the treatment of emotional stress consists in showing the patient precisely what maturity means in the handling of everyday living, and then showing him a practical discipline for carrying on his living with a passable degree of maturity.

In contrast, the therapy of traditional psychiatry consists quite largely of digging into the personal history and the half-buried past, a very interesting though, in my opinion, not a very fruitful method of treatment. It does afford the therapist an excellent idea of the particular variety of immaturity a patient has, but this is a matter which can be determined fairly readily, without hours spent on a psychiatric couch. Being interested mainly in the past, the traditional psychiatrist often prefers to do very little about the present or the future.

The learning-maturity concept, on the other hand, insists that, regardless of the omissions and commissions of the past, a person has to *start in the present* to acquire some maturity so that the future may be better than the past. The present and the future depend on learning new habits and new ways of looking at old problems. There simply isn't any future in digging continually into the past.

Instead of recreating the past, as does the conditioning concept, the learning-maturity concept emphasizes an improved approach for the present and future.

➤ The Common Denominator in Emotionally Induced Illness

The starting point in the treatment of E. I. I. becomes simple and clear when one realizes that the underlying emotional problem has the same common denominator in every patient. This common denominator is that the patient has forgotten how, or probably never learned how, to control his *present* thinking to produce *enjoyment*. Constant fear, anxiety, apprehension, irritation, frustration, and discouragement absolutely preclude the possibility of enjoyment. Emotional stress can be helped *only by learning* to react to situations RIGHT NOW with equanimity, courage, determination, and cheerfulness. The person who learns to handle the majority of life situations with equanimity, courage, determination, and cheerfulness has taken a long step into maturity. Beyond this step there remains the development of unselfish cooperativeness and good judgment to make maturity fairly complete.

My method of therapy places the patient on the enjoyment principle by a conditioned reflex through conscious thought control, by substituting equanimity, courage, determination, and cheerfulness, whenever anxiety, apprehension, and so on, begin to make their appearances. This substitution is done by conscious thought control until habit can eventually take over. Such substitution is what people with emotional stasis are doing habitually all the time.

➡ The Practical Application of the Common Denominator and the Learning-Maturity Concept

The point of greatest practical difference between the traditional adequate psychotherapy and the learning-maturity method is this: adequate psychotherapy requires hours and hours of the doctor's time and can, therefore, be used only on an extremely small fraction of patients who need therapy; the learning-maturity method can be applied in ways that require practically none of the doctor's time.

How can the learning-maturity method be applied without hours of the doctor's time?

First, because maturity in one person is the same thing as maturity in another person, and second, because there is the same common denominator in every person with emotionally induced illness, the course and procedure of therapy *is the same in every patient*, regardless of how their problems may differ in detail.

The essential thing to show patients is how they may henceforth meet the ordinary life situations with maturity and emotional stasis, and how they may introduce enjoyment into the present moment. This can be done in the same way for everyone. Therapy for emotionally induced illness can be standardized to a single pattern and yet help practically 100 per cent of the patients. If one can develop a system of instruction that will help *one* patient develop maturity and emotional stasis, the same system would work for almost any other patient.

For the past 20 years I have tried various methods and various techniques, working always with this requirement in mind: Because there are so many patients with E. I. I., the doctor must have a method that does not require much of his time. I submit that *unless a method meets this criterion, it is useless in medical practice.*

One method that at first seemed to promise well was group therapy. Ten, 25, 50, even 75 patients would meet periodically for orientation lectures, followed by general group discussion. But this grew to a point where I was spending three hours every night with such groups. This was not saving the doctor's time and it was a grueling program!

The results of group therapy were encouraging, but not too satisfactory. Much still remained to be given the patient in private sessions.

After several false starts with sound alone, I finally tried an audiovisual demonstration, using wire recordings, and later tape recordings, coupled with colored slides projected on a screen. Almost at once patient response indicated that this was it!

The method was perfected so that one patient, and his spouse, could receive instruction in private. What this method lacked by not having the doctor talking directly to the patient was more than compensated by the thoughtful care that could go into the preparation of a tape recording far superior to an off-the-cuff lecture, plus the additional interest of slides on a screen giving point and interest to the demonstration. The doctor saw the patient briefly before and after each audiovisual demonstration.

Here was a method which worked during the day while the doctor was attending his other patients. Bit by bit the audiovisual demonstrations were pieced together, changed here and altered there, until they developed a hitting power that far exceeded the group therapy sessions. The present demonstrations can admittedly be vastly improved upon, and, indeed, they are constantly being added to and changed.

The audiovisual sessions are attended by the patient and his spouse at weekly intervals. He sees the doctor for a period of five minutes before and after each session, so that the doctor may make certain that the patient is being suitably oriented. The tape recordings present essentially the same material contained in this book, greatly augmented by the visual aid of the screen projections.

During the past six years, thousands of patients have attended these therapeutic sessions. The majority have either been cured of their ailment, or have been shown how to tolerate their symptoms. Most of them have been shown how to live happily. The doctor, too, benefits by removing his greatest worry and care, which is "How can I possibly bring effective help to these scores of people with emotionally induced illness?" The layman cannot possibly appreciate what a tremendous burden functional disease produces for the doctor. The doctor needs a method of therapy as much as does the patient.

Having seen what can be accomplished by audiovisual sessions utilizing the learning-maturity concept, and failing to see how the tremendous number of patients can be given the necessary therapy in any other way, I am of the opinion that eventually this system, or some modification of it, *must* become the universally accepted method of treating emotionally induced illness.

➡ *A Comparison of the Learning-Maturity Method and "Adequate Psychotherapy"*

Adequate psychotherapy for E. I. I. consists of three distinct phases, the period of explanation, the period of ventilation, the period of education.

The emphasis is placed on the period of ventilation; the

period of explanation is very sketchy and often unconvincing; the period of education varies in intensity with various psychiatrists. Some leave it out altogether.

Psychoanalysis consists only of the period of ventilation. The analyst considers a period of education entirely superfluous.

The learning-maturity method by audiovisual presentation emphasizes the period of explanation and the period of education. The period of ventilation is turned into a period of demonstration.

The period of explanation. The initial step, in both adequate psychotherapy and in the learning-maturity method, is to explain to the patient that he has emotionally induced illness, and to give him some idea of how E. I. I. works.

The adequate psychotherapist has considerable trouble in doing this because his explanations are exceedingly ephemeral, and leave the average patient completely unconvinced.

As an example: a patient of mine who was seen by a psychiatrist was given this explanation of his diarrhea: "You hate your mother-in-law, and you would like nothing better than to have her out of your life. Your diarrhea is your body's organ-language of that repressed desire." To the patient that sounded pretty weak. He was not convinced that his diarrhea had anything to do with his mother-in-law, especially when his diarrhea did not stop after his mother-in-law had been killed in an accident (with which the patient had nothing to do).

Admittedly the man's mother-in-law had much to do with the emotional stress which was manifesting itself in his colon, but to give the explanation that the body is acting out a phrase of language, which the mind dare not express, is, in my opinion, just as silly as it sounds. It sounded silly to the patient.

Another symbolic psychiatric explanation is, "You feel a lump in your throat because that is your body's expression of the fact that you have things in your life you can't swallow." There is, of course, a connection between the "things in your life" and the lump; but why can't the explanation be factual, that is to say, physiological, instead of merely figurative?

It is much easier to convince patients that they have E. I. I. if the explanation is physiological, as in the first part of this book. After the audiovisual sessions on explanation, the patient usually says, "Sure, you were describing me all the time. Why didn't someone tell me before how this worked?"

We know, today, what the mechanism of E. I. I. is. Why not use it? In fairness, it must be noted that psychiatrists are turning more and more to physiologic explanations of the emotion-symptom relationship. But many of them still rely on the hokus-pokus of symbolism.

The period of ventilation. Traditional psychiatrists, and especially psychoanalysts, place their main emphasis on the part of their therapy they term "ventilation," which consists in having the patient talk about himself.

The ventilative sessions of an hour each, at weekly intervals, extend from weeks to years, depending on how deeply buried the subconscious material happens to be.

From such ventilation, the psychiatrist hopes to have the patient uncover the mainspring of his illness, the theory being that emotional stress is due to repressed and buried complexes that tend to disappear as soon as the patient knows of their presence and significance. The main objection to this theory is that it does not often work; it does not often produce a cure of the patient's emotional stress.

In the audiovisual presentation of the learning-maturity method there is obviously no place for ventilation. Instead of listening to the patient ventilate, as in "adequate psychotherapy," the doctor ventilates for the patient. In the audiovisual sessions, as in this book, the patient is presented with the chief situational and personality factors that produce emotional stress He has time to compare his own situation with the hypothetical ones presented during the sessions; he analyzes himself and realizes that perhaps what he has always considered normal for himself is, after all abnormal.

Very often, a person who has attended several audiovisual sessions will voluntarily reveal a situation in his life that he had been hiding. If the patient doesn't voluntarily bring me an assay of himself after a reasonable number of sessions, I ask him, "Now that you have seen the kind of thing that produces E. I. I. in most people, what do you think is doing it in you?" If he doesn't have an immediate answer, I ask him to bring it with him before he attends the next session.

The period of education. After the explanatory and ventilative periods, the psychotherapist usually discusses, with the patient, ways and means of alleviating his difficulties. This period of education is by no means universally used by all psychiatrists. Many psychiatrists do not give the patient any directive program and believe educational efforts are useless. Their emphasis, of course, is on the cathartic effect of the ventilative period.

The learning-maturity concept emphasizes the educative period. The main effort is *not* to dig up the past but to show the patient how he may go about acquiring the qualities that will make his present and future more endurable and satisfactory than his past.

A person is what he is because of the sum total of influences that he has met in the past. Whatever those influences were does not preclude the application of new influences and new learning patterns now or in the future. If a poor swimmer is shown how, the chances are he can be a better swimmer. Once in a great while, of course, there will be someone who just can't learn to swim, but the majority can be helped.

The *final* know-how for developing maturity and emotional stasis we do not yet have; it is something that will have to be acquired through trial and error. However, there is already quite a bit we do know; let us begin to apply that.

INDEX

INDEX